China's Rare Earth Industry and Export Regime: Economic and Trade Implications for the United States

Wayne M. Morrison
Specialist in Asian Trade and Finance

Rachel Tang
Analyst in Asian Affairs

April 30, 2012

Congressional Research Service

7-5700

www.crs.gov

R42510

Summary

Over the past few years, the Chinese government has implemented a number of policies to tighten its control over the production and export of "rare earths"—a unique group of 17 metal elements on the periodic table that exhibit a range of special properties, such as magnetism, luminescence, and strength. Rare earths are important to a number of high technology industries, including renewable energy and various defense systems.

China's position as the world's dominant producer and supplier of rare earths (97% of total output) and its policies to limit exports have raised concerns among many in Congress, especially given the importance of rare earths to a variety of U.S. commercial industries (e.g., hybrid and conventional autos, oil and gas, energy-efficient lighting, advanced electronics, chemicals, and medical equipment), as well as to U.S. defense industries that produce various weapon systems. Many are concerned that rising rare earth prices could undermine the global competitiveness of many U.S. firms (lowering their production and employment), impede technological innovation, and raise prices for U.S. consumers. Others are concerned that China's virtual monopoly over rare earths could be used as leverage against major rare earth importers, such as the United States, Japan, and the European Union (EU).

To many observers, China's rare earth policies are part of a complex web of Chinese government industrial policies that seek to promote the development of domestic industries deemed essential to economic modernization. In the late 1980s, the United States was the global leader in rare earth production. However, preferential policies by the Chinese government and lax environmental standards there quickly enabled China to become a dominant, low-cost producer of rare earths by the late 1990s. Many analysts contend that China's recent actions to consolidate its rare earth production and restrict exports are intended to promote the development of domestic downstream industries, especially those engaged in high technology and green technology industries, by ensuring their access to adequate and low-cost supplies of rare earths. It is further argued that China's rare earth export policies are intended to induce foreign rare earth users to move their operations to China, and subsequently, to transfer technology to Chinese firms. China denies that its rare earth policies are political, discriminatory, or protectionist, but rather, are intended to address environmental concerns in China and to better manage and conserve limited resources.

On March 13, 2012, the United States, Japan, and the EU jointly initiated a World Trade Organization (WTO) dispute settlement case against China's restrictive policies on rare earths and two other minerals. This case was brought shortly after the United States largely prevailed in a similar WTO case brought against China over its export restrictions on nine raw materials. The Obama Administration has also sought to devise strategies to deal with rare earth shortages, including the development of a diversified global rare earth supply chain, the development of alternative materials, and more efficient use of rare earth, including recycling. A number of bills have been introduced in Congress that seek to address U.S. rare earths shortages. A major issue for Congress raised by the rare earths dispute is whether U.S. trade policy can effectively respond to China's industrial policies that may negatively impact U.S. economic interests, either through the WTO or other means.

This report examines the economic and trade implications of China's rare earth policies for the United States.

Contents

Figures

Tables

Contacts

Introduction

China is a major global producer of many raw materials, and, in some cases, a dominant producer. Particular concern has been raised in the United States and elsewhere over China's near-monopoly in the production of "rare earths"—a group of 17 elements whose unique properties make them critical in a variety of advanced technologies. Due to their special properties of magnetism, luminescence, and strength, rare earths are widely used in high-technology and clean energy products, as well as in military weapon systems.[1] According to one analyst, rare earth elements "are critical to hundreds of high tech applications, many of which define our modern way of life. Without rare earth elements, much of the world's modern technology would be vastly different, and many applications would not be possible."[2]

The Chinese government has made the development of its rare earth resources a top priority since the 1980s. In 1992, Chinese leader Deng Xiaoping reportedly said, "China's rare earth resources can be likened in importance to the Middle East's oil. They have immense strategic significance and we must certainly deal with rare earths issues with care, unleashing the advantages they bring."[3] In 1999, Chinese President Jiang Zemin reportedly wrote: "Improve the development and applications of rare earth, and change the resource advantage into economic superiority."[4] Government support for the rare earth industry, low labor costs, and lax environmental standards enabled China to become the world's dominant producer of rare earths, estimated to be the source of over 97% of the global supply.

In recent years, China has been restructuring its domestic rare earth industry while putting more restrictions on rare earth exports, which has greatly affected the price and quantity of rare earths available in the global market. This has caused concern among businesses and foreign governments about potential business risks and geopolitical implications. Such concerns became more acute when China reportedly suspended shipments of rare earths to Japan, due to a months-long diplomatic crisis with Japan in September of 2010.[5]

China's rare earth policies have raised concerns among many in Congress because rare earths are important to a number of U.S. industries, including high technology (such as advanced electronics and medical equipment) and green technology (such as hybrid cars and wind turbines). In addition, U.S. defense industries rely on rare earths for a variety of weapon systems. China's export restrictions over the past two years have disrupted supplies and sharply raised prices for rare earths outside China. Some Members contend that China's export restrictions on rare earths are intended to give domestic Chinese downstream users a competitive advantage (because of the

---

[1] Pul-Kwan Tse, *China's Rare Earth Industry*, U.S. Geological Survey, Open File Report 2011-1042, p.1. These 17 rare earth elements consists of 15 lanthanide elements (atomic numbers 57-71) and two elements with similar chemical characteristics, scandium (Sc) and yttrium (Y). The 15 lanthanide elements are: Lanthanum (La); Cerium (Ce); Praseodymium (Pr); Neodymium (Nd); Promethium (Pm); Samarium (Sm); Europium (Eu); Gadolinium (Gd); Terbium (Tb); Dysprosium (Dy); Holmium (Ho); Erbium (Er); Thulium (Tm); Ytterbium (Yb); and Lutetium (Lu).

[2] Cindy Hurst, *China's Rare Earth Elements Industry: What Can the West Learn?* Institute for the Analysis of Global Security, March 2010, p.3.

[3] Reuters, "China's Dream for Rare Earths Rests on Grim Costs," November 3, 2010.

[4] *Foreign Policy Magazine*, "Is China Making a Rare Earth Power Play?," September 23, 2010.

[5] *The Wall Street Journal*, "China Denies Halting Rare Earth Exports to Japan," September 23, 2010; *The Telegraph*, "Rare Earths: Why China Is Cutting Exports Crucial to Western Technologies," March 19, 2011.

---

secured access to rare earth supply and the significant disparity between domestic and external rare earth prices) over foreign competitors, and/or to induce foreign users of rare earths to move their production facilities to China. Members have also expressed concerns that China's virtual monopoly of rare earths may impact U.S. economic and security interests because it makes many U.S. commercial and defense industries vulnerable to supply shortages and higher prices as a result of future Chinese restrictions that could occur for economic, as well as political, reasons. Several bills have been introduced in Congress to address these concerns, including H.R. 618, H.R. 952, H.R. 1314, H.R. 1388, H.R. 1540, H.R. 2011, H.R. 2184, H.R. 2284, S. 1113, and S. 1270.[6] In the House, a congressional caucus on rare earths was established in late 2011 to push for reestablishing a domestic rare earth supply chain in order to reduce U.S. dependence on China.

This report provides an overview of the U.S. dispute with China over its restrictions of rare earth exports. It examines the level of U.S. rare earth trade with China, how Chinese policies have affected rare earth prices for U.S. firms, possible motivations behind China's restrictions of rare earth exports, and how the United States and other major users of rare earths have responded, including a WTO dispute settlement case brought by the United States, Japan, and the EU in March 2012 against China over its rare earths restrictions. In addition, the report also examines China's rare earth industry and government policies – their evolution, recent developments, and effectiveness in meeting the government's goals (such as consolidating production, addressing pollution, and halting illegal mining).

This report does not provide extensive discussion of rare earths from a resource supply chain perspective, nor from a national defense angle. For additional information on these topics, see CRS Report R41347, *Rare Earth Elements: The Global Supply Chain*, by Marc Humphries; and CRS Report R41744, *Rare Earth Elements in National Defense: Background, Oversight Issues, and Options for Congress*, by Valerie Bailey Grasso.

Background on Rare Earths

Contrary to the name, rare earths are not "rare." Rather, they are relatively abundant in the earth's crust. At the same time, however, they are highly scattered and are usually found mixed together in other deposits, which makes it difficult to find rare earths in a concentration high enough to be mined and separated economically. When rare earths are extracted from the mine, the ore containing the rare earths must go through complex separation processes to produce each individual element. It is the separation process that largely drives the cost of rare earth production.[7]

The 17 rare earth elements are often divided into two groups: light and heavy rare earth elements.[8] Two of the largest rare earth mines outside China, namely, Mountain Pass in the

---

[6] In addition, S. 948, S. 1220, S. 1294, and S. 1351 require, among other things, that the Secretary of the Interior conduct a study related to raw materials needed for the manufacture of plug-in electric drive vehicles, batteries, and other components for plug-in electric drive vehicles, and for the infrastructure needed to support plug-in electric drive vehicles. Such raw materials would likely include rare earths.

[7] Testimony by Mark A. Smith, CEO of Molycorp Minerals, LLC, before the House Science and Technology Committee, Subcommittee on Investigations and Oversight on March 16, 2010.

[8] U.S. Geological Survey, "The Principal Rare Earth Elements Deposits of the United States, a Summary of Domestic Deposits and a Global Perspective," Scientific Investigations Report 2010-5220, November 16, 2010. Traditionally, the (continued...)

United States and Mount Weld in Australia, contain mainly light rare earths. Many electronic products require heavy rare earths to perform more efficiently. Currently, China is the only country that can supply a significant amount of both light and heavy rare earths, and is likely to remain the major supplier of heavy rare earths in the near future.[9]

Rare earth deposits often contain radioactive elements, which means separating the metals requires costly and strenuous processes that produce a number of toxic pollutants and hazardous waste material. When the Mountain Pass mine in the United States was operating at full capacity in the 1990s, it produced as much as 850 gallons of salty wastewater per minute, which also contained radioactive thorium and uranium. The hazardous materials built up as scale inside the pipe that delivered the wastewater to evaporation ponds 11 miles away. Several times in the 1990s, cleaning operations caused the pipeline to burst, spilling hazardous waste into the desert. Molycorp, then a unit of the oil company Unocal, was ordered by the state of California to clean up the waste. In 2002, the already struggling Molycorp ran out of space to store its waste and failed to secure a permit to build a new storage facility. As a result, the mine shut down. Chevron's acquisition of Unocal in 2005 and other developments will be discussed later in this report.[10]

The list of rare earth applications is extensive and these applications can be found in many industries. Rare earths are used in petroleum refining and as diesel additives in the oil industry; they are important to the automotive industry because of their wide application in catalytic converters, hybrid vehicle batteries, motors and generators; they are used by the electronics industry to make hard disk drives and cell phones; and they are used in powerful magnets in wind turbines (see **Figure 1**).

While rare earth applications in high-tech have existed for decades, it is their application in clean energy technologies and defense systems that has brought global attention to rare earths. Rare earth metals' super magnetic strength allows for extraordinary miniaturization of components, which have important military applications. For example, the fins that steer precision bombs have samarium-cobalt permanent magnet motors; the solid-state lasers used to designate targets use neodymium.[11]

(...continued)

REE are divided into two groups on the basis of atomic weight: the light rare earth elements are lanthanum through europium (atomic numbers = 57 through 63); and the heavy rare earth elements are gadolinium through lutetium (atomic numbers = 64 through 71). Yttrium (atomic number = 39), although light in atomic weight, is included with the heavy REE group because of its common chemical and physical affiliations with the heavy REE in nature.

[9] Statement of W. David Menzie, Chief of Global Minerals Analysis, National Minerals Information Center, U.S. Geological Survey, before the U.S.-China Economic and Security Review Commission hearing on "China's Global Quest for Resources and Implications for the United States," January 26, 2012.

[10] Katherine Bourzac, *Technology Review*, "The Rare-Earth Crisis" (May/June 2011), pp. 61-62. According to a U.S. Geological Survey report, "The Principal Rare Earth Elements Deposits of the U.S. – a Summary of Domestic Deposits and a Global Perspective," the Mountain Pass rare earth mines in Californian used to supply most of the light rare earths consumed domestically and by other industrialized countries, until 1998, when production started to decrease due to competition from China.

[11] *The Wall Street Journal*, "China Hold on Metals Worries Washington," September 23, 2010.

Figure 1. Applications of Rare Earths

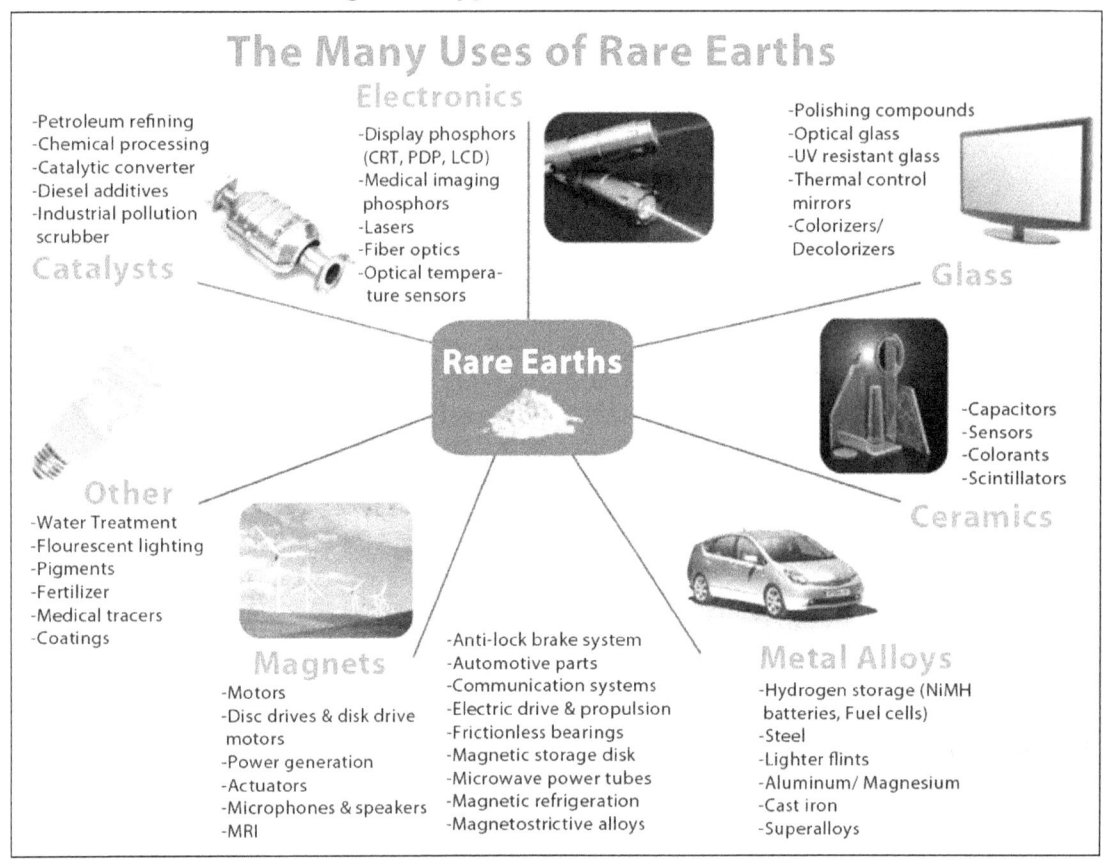

Source: Molycorp Inc. company website (www.molycorp.com), as viewed on February 21, 2012.

Overview of U.S. Rare Earth Trade

China has become the world's dominant producer, user, and exporter of rare earth elements. China's trade data indicate that the value of its rare earth exports in 2011 was $3.4 billion.[12] According to the U.S. Geological Survey (USGS), China currently accounts for an estimated 97.3% of global mine production of rare earth elements (compared to 27% in 1990).[13] The United States, like many other countries, has become dependent on China for rare earth materials, from oxides, metals, and alloys to permanent magnets and finished products, as illustrated by the following data and figures:[14]

---

[12] Data calculated by CRS using the USITC Dataweb, based on China's 2011 harmonized tariff schedule (HTS) classification of raw earths listed in the publication: "Rare Earths an Update: A Fresh Look at the Supplier(s), the Buyers, and the Trade Rules," by the Law Offices of Stewart and Stewart, 2011. Note, U.S. and Chinese HTS classifications of commodities that constitute "rare earths" differ significantly.

[13] U.S. Geological Survey, *Mineral Commodities Survey, Rare Earth, 2011*, available at http://minerals.usgs.gov/minerals/pubs/commodity/rare_earths/mcs-2011-raree.pdf. Other producers include Brazil, the Commonwealth of Independent States, and Malaysia. Note, estimates of mine production data of rare earths for various countries are not available. The United States did not mine rare earths in 2011, but is estimated to have 13 million tons of rare earth reserves (about 12% of estimated global reserves) from prior mining operations.

[14] The United States is believed to be the world's second largest importer of rare earths after Japan. China is the largest (continued...)

- As indicated in **Figure 2**, Japan was by far China's largest export market for rare earth exports in 2011 (according to Chinese trade data), based on value (at 66% of total), followed by the United States (7%), France (6%), Germany (5%), Hong Kong (4%), and South Korea (3%).[15]

- According to the U.S. International Trade Commission (USITC), the value of U.S. rare earth imports from the world totaled $860 million in 2011, up from $94 million in 2002, an 815% increase (see **Figure 3**).[16] The value of U.S. rare earth imports from China in 2011 was $523 million, which was 0.13% of total U.S. imports from China.[17] From 2002 to 2011, the value of U.S. rare earth imports from China rose by 1,376%. From 2010 to 2011, the value of U.S. rare earth imports from China increased by 305%.

- The U.S. dependence on China for its rare earth imports is significant when measured by quantity (i.e., kilograms or metric tons). From 2002 to 2011, the quantity of U.S. rare earth imports from China as a percent of total U.S. rare earth imports averaged 78.3%. The share of U.S. rare earth imports from China fell from 79.1% in 2010 to 53.5% in 2011. This was largely the result of a 50.8% drop in the level of U.S. rare earth imports from China and a 107.6% increase in the quantity of U.S. rare earth imports from Japan.[18]

- The quantity of U.S. rare earth imports from China has fallen sharply in recent years, from a high of 24,513 metric tons in 2006 to 6,884 metric tons in 2011 – a 71.9% drop (see **Figure 4**). From 2010 to 2011, total U.S. imports of rare earths dropped from 17,707 metric tons to 12,911 metric tons (a 27.1% drop), while imports of rare earths from China fell from 14,005 metric tons to 6,884 metric tons (a 50.8% drop). Rising prices of imported Chinese rare earths and the lingering effects of the global economic slowdown, including in the United States, were likely the main causes of the drop in U.S. rare earth imports.

- Prices for imported Chinese rare earths have risen significantly over the past few years. As seen in **Figure 5**, the average U.S customs value per metric ton of rare earth imports from China rose from $3,111 in 2002 to $76,239 in 2011, a 2,432% increase. The increased prices for rare earth imports from China was particularly acute in 2011, when average prices jumped 723% in one year.[19]

(...continued)
user of rare earths, followed by Japan and the United States.

[15] Source: Global Trade Atlas using China's 2011 HTS classification of rare earths and Chinese trade data.

[16] For U.S. data on rare earth trade, the source is the U.S. Geological Survey's description of "rare earth metals, compounds, etc." and their corresponding categories in the U.S. Harmonized Tariff Schedule (HTS). These include HTS numbers 2612.20.0000, 2805.30.0000, 2846.10.0000, 2846.90.2010, 2846.90.2050, 2846.90.4000, 2846.90.8000, and 3606.90.3000. These classifications do not include U.S. imports of manufactured products that contain rare earths, such as high performance magnets, hybrid batteries, consumer electronic products, etc. Thus, the trade data may understate the importance of rare earths to the U.S. economy as a whole and various U.S. industrial sectors that use imported inputs that contain rare earths in their production.

[17] U.S. exports of rare earths in 2011 were $316 million. Japan was the largest destination of U.S. rare earth exports (accounting for 33.6% of total), followed by Thailand and Estonia.

[18] Since Japan does not mine rare earths, these commodities must have been mined elsewhere, possibly China.

[19] These data represent changes in rare earth prices as a whole.

Figure 2. Major Destinations of China's Rare Earth Exports in 2011

(% of total)

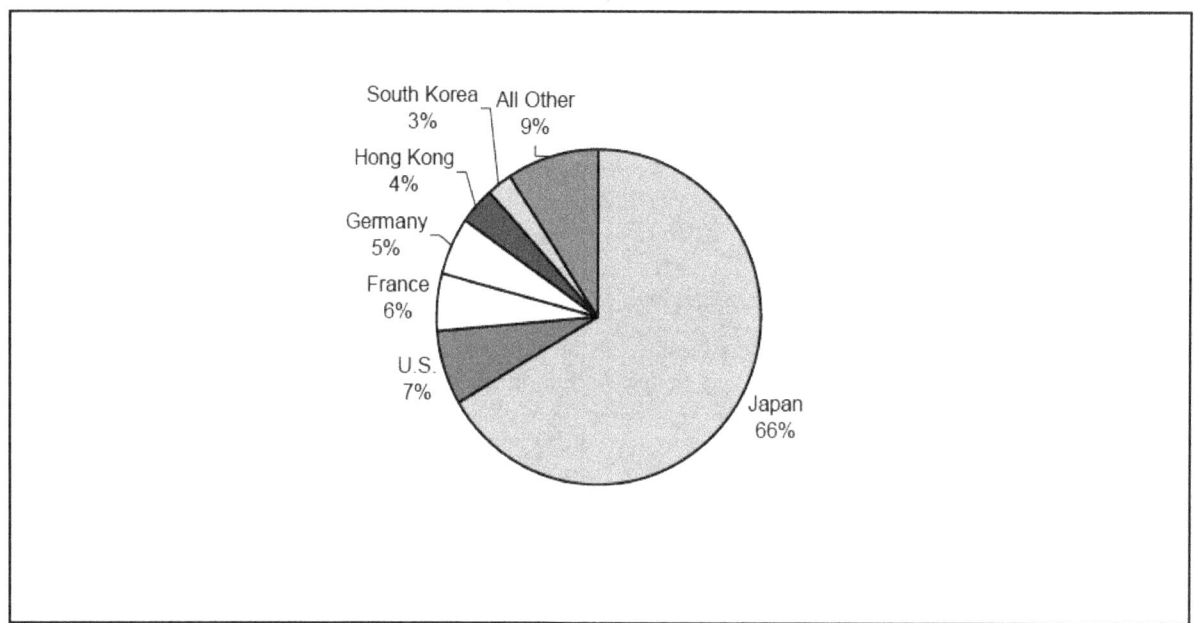

Source: Global Trade Atlas.

Notes: Based on China's HTS classification of rare earth in 2011.

Figure 3. Total Value of U.S. Rare Earth Imports: 2002-2011

($ millions)

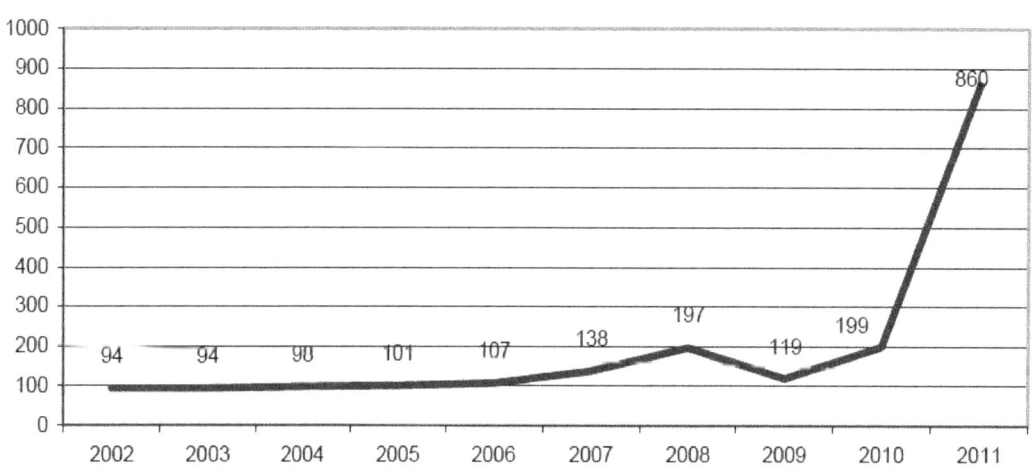

Source: USITC DataWeb.

Notes: Based on the U.S. Geological Survey's classification of rare earths.

Figure 4. Quantity of U.S. Rare Earth Imports from China and the World: 2002-2011

(metric tons)

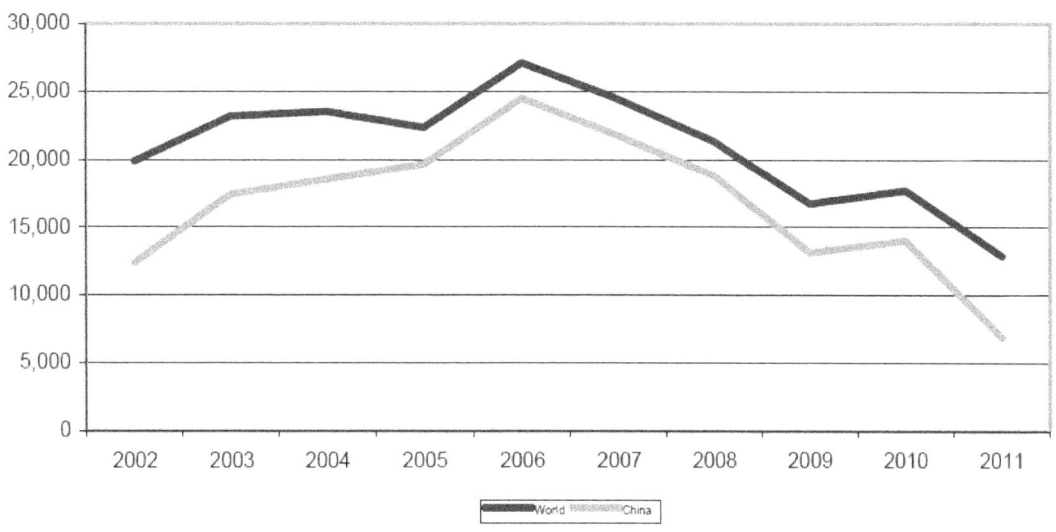

Source:. USITC Dataweb.

Note: : Rare earth categories as defined by the U.S. Geological Survey.

Figure 5. Customs Value Per Metric Ton of U.S. Rare Earth Imports From China: 2002-2011

($)

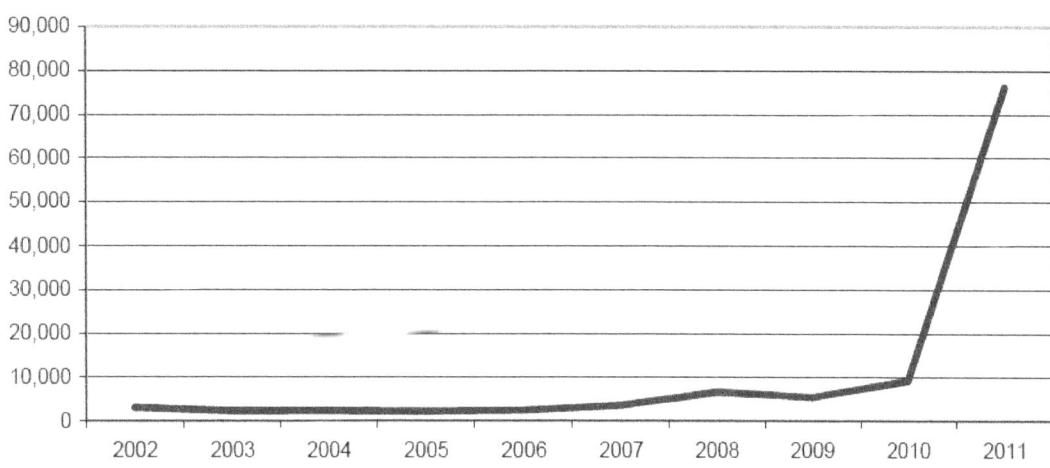

Source: USITC Dataweb.

Note: Rare earth categories as defined by the U.S. Geological Survey. The data represents average prices for all rare earth imports. Prices for individual rare earth commodities differ significantly.

China as the World's Dominant Rare Earth Supplier

The United States was the leading producer of rare earths from the 1940s to the mid-1980s, when it provided the majority of rare earth minerals to the rest the world from the Mountain Pass mine in California. During the 1990s, Chinese rare earths production increased drastically and, according to Jeffery A. Green:

> … flooded the market by more than tripling the previous world supply of the materials. During this time, Chinese rare earth-producing firms were largely unprofitable but were allowed to survive through direct and indirect support by the Chinese government. This backing enable China's rare earth industry to continue to mine and export these materials at prices far below the actual costs of production.

> With the additional industrial advantage of a low labor cost, questionable environmental standards, and export taxes, the impact of these efforts were swift and dramatic: within 20 years China went from producing roughly one-third to nearly all of the world's supply of rare earths. Mines in the United Sates and elsewhere, unable to remain profitable against cheap Chinese exports, went out of business.[20]

Rare Earth Resources in China

There are three known and verified locations where high concentration of rare earths exist: Baiyun Obo of Inner Mongolia, China; Mountain Pass, California, where Molycorp's mine is located and production has restarted; and Mt. Weld, Australia, which has a rich ore deposit but needs necessary infrastructure to begin mining, separation, and transportation to market.

China is rich in rare earth resources and, according to some estimates, has half of the world's total rare earth reserves.[21] Known in China as "industrial vitamins," or in early years as "industrial MSG," a variety of rare earth deposits have been discovered in more than 20 provinces and "autonomous" regions in China,[22] The largest rare earth reserve is Baiyun Obo (also known as Bayan Obo) in the Chinese autonomous region of Inner Mongolia, accounting for more than 83% of China's rare earth reserves and about half of all rare earths output in China. The other regions with significant rare earths resources are Shandong (7.7%), Sichuan (3%), and a number of provinces in southern China (3%),[23] as illustrated in **Figure 7**.

It is worth noting that the rare earth deposits in Inner Mongolia in northern China are mainly light rare earths. The more scarce and sought-after heavy rare earths are concentrated in southern China, especially in Jiangxi, Guangdong, Fujian, Guangxi, and Hunan provinces.[24] Currently,

---

[20] Testimony by Jeffery A. Green before the U.S.- China Economic and Security Review Commission Hearing on "China's Global Quest for Resources and Implications for the United States" on January 26, 2012.

[21] Estimates of China's rare earth reserves as a percent of global total varies. The U.S. Geological Survey estimates this level at 50% (Source USGS, *Minerals Information, Rare Earths*, 2012), while China's own estimate puts it at 36% (Source: *People's Daily Online*, March 19, 2012).

[22] Pui-Kwan Tse, *China's Rare Earth Industry*, U.S. Geological Survey, Open File Report 2011-1042, p.1.

[23] Su Wenqing, *Analysis: The Economics and Policy of China's Rare Earths Industry* (Beijing, China: Chinese Finance & Economy Publishing House, May 2009 ed.), pp. 84. CRS used the Chinese-language version of the book.

[24] Xinhua, *Outlook Weekly,* Issue No. 201130. http://news.sina.com.cn/c/sd/2011-07-23/195622864615.shtml. CRS used the original Chinese-language version of the report.

China is the only country that can provide significant supplies of both light and heavy rare earths. Rare earths from the Mountain Pass mine in California and the Mount Weld mine in western Australia contain, predominantly, light rare earths.

China's Rare Earth Industry

China's rare earth production started in the late 1950s, in the Chinese region of Inner Mongolia, where the Baiyun Obo iron ore deposit was discovered in 1927. It is by far the world's largest rare earth mine, where rare earth minerals are recovered as byproducts during iron ore mining. Spread over a minerals-rich area of 48 km^2, the total reserve of Baiyun Obo is estimated to be about 36 million tons (measured by rare earths oxides (REO) equivalent).[25] The iron ore deposit in Baiyun Obo has been mined primarily for steel making by Baotou Iron and Steel, (also known as Baotou Steel or Bao Gang), a major state-owned steel producer in northern China. Baotou Research Institute of Rare Earths (formerly Baotou Metallurgical Research Institute), now the biggest and most prominent rare earth research facility in China, was established in 1963.[26]

Baotou Steel's Rare Earth Hi-Tech (Group) Company, the largest (and state-controlled) rare earth producer in China, produces 55,000 metric tons of processed rare earths a year. This accounts for nearly half of China's production, or, about 44% of global rare earth production.[27]

In the late 1970s, annual rare earth production in China was just slightly over 1,000 tons (REO equivalent), which were mainly a byproduct from the iron ore tailings (waste materials from the iron extraction process). At that time, rare earth production in southern China was still at the initial stage, with an annual yield of 60 tons.[28] Chinese rare earth production remained insignificant for several decades until the 1980s. During that era, China's rare earths industry was represented by three state-owned factories.[29]

In the 1980s, rare earth production in China started to take off due to improved techniques, strong demand, and more market-oriented economic policies. In 1985, China introduced export rebates for rare earth products, which were abolished 20 years later to curb exports. In 1986, China surpassed the United States to be the world's top producer and a major supplier of rare earths, a title held by China ever since.[30]

---

[25] Baiyun Obo iron ore deposit website: http://www.byebtk.com.cn/bytk/About.asp?ID=29, as viewed on January 24, 2012; T.K.S. Murphy and T.K. Mukherjee, *Rare Earths: Occurrence, Production and Applications* (Technology Information, Forecasting and Assessment Council (TIFAC) and The Indian Institute of Metals (IIM), 2002 ed.), p. 57.

[26] Baotou Research Institute of Rare Earths (BRIRE) was under the former Ministry of Metallurgical Industry until 1992, when it joined Baotou Iron and Steel (Bao Gang) Group Corp. BRIRE website: http://www.brire.com/, as viewed on January 24, 2012.

[27] Ibid. Baotou Steel Rare Earth Hi-Tech Co. is also the largest rare earth producer in the world.

[28] Su Wenqing, *Analysis: The Economics and Policy of China's Rare Earths Industry* (Beijing, China: Chinese Finance & Economy Publishing House, May 2009 ed.), pp. 120-122, p.137, and p.151. CRS used the original Chinese-language version of the book.

[29] Xinhua, *Outlook Weekly,* Issue No. 201130, http://news.sina.com.cn/c/sd/2011-07-23/195622864615.shtml. The three state-owned factories were Baotou Rare Earths Factory No. 3, Shanghai Yuelong Chemicals Factory, and Zhujiang Metallurgical Factory. CRS used the original Chinese-language version of the report.

[30] Su Wenqing, *Analysis: The Economics and Policy of China's Rare Earths Industry,* (Beijing, China: Chinese Finance & Economy Publishing House, May 2009 ed.), pp. 120-122, p.137, and p.151.

In the 1990s, high profit margin in the rare earth business started to attract many start-up enterprises in China. The competition became so fierce that rare earth prices were pushed downward due to production overcapacity, even as exports increased. Between 2002 and 2005, reportedly, average rare earth prices in China dropped to about US$5.50 per kilogram, a historic low.[31] Largely because rare earths from China became so abundant and at such low prices that other suppliers were unable to compete with Chinese prices and supply, most of the world's mines outside China were closed by the early 2000s, including the mine in Mountain Pass, California. At the same time, China invested heavily in rare earth refining and production technologies. It developed cheaper processes that used hydrochloric instead of nitric acid and managed to refine extractions to higher purity, and reportedly better quality, than in the United States.[32]

Data on China's export of rare earths are shown in **Figure 6**, based on China's 2011 tariff schedule classification of rare earths, which has changed over time. These data indicate that China's rare earth exports rose sharply from 1995 to 2003, but have sharply declined since then (especially after 2008).[33]

Figure 6. China's Rare Earth Exports: 1995-2011

(thousands of metric tons)

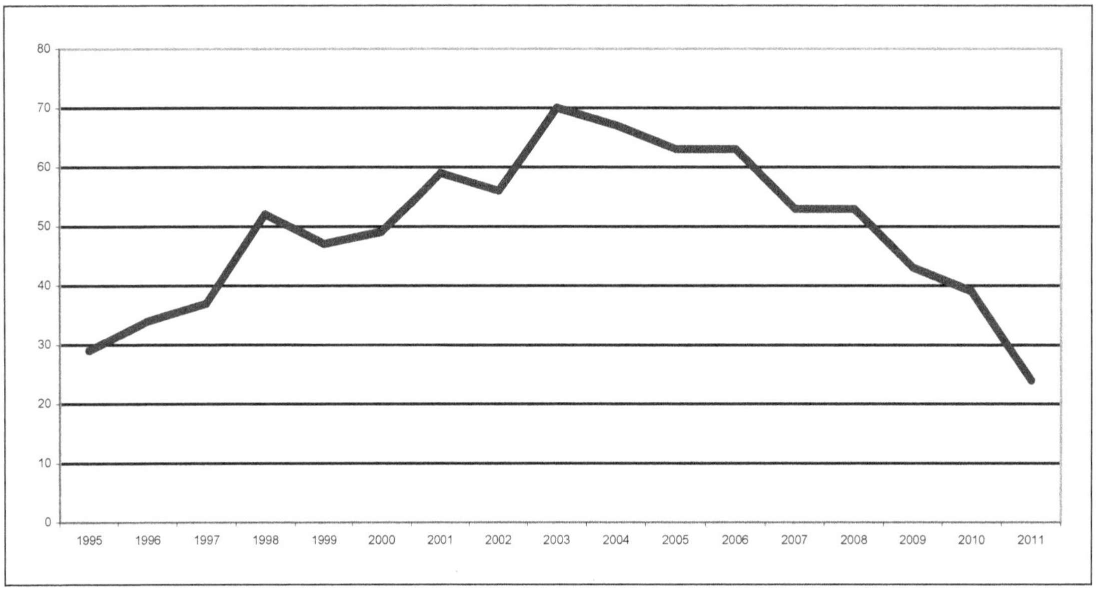

Source: Global Trade Atlas.

Notes: Calculated according to China's HTS classification of rare earths in 2011.

---

[31] Ibid.

[32] *The Telegraph,* "Rare Earths: Why China Is Cutting Exports Crucial to Western Technologies," March 19, 2011,

[33] Data calculated by CRS using the USITC Dataweb, based on China's 2011 harmonized tariff schedule classification of raw earths listed in the publication: "Rare Earths an Update: A Fresh Look at the Supplier(s), the Buyers, and the Trade Rules," by the Law Offices of Stewart and Stewart, 2011, at http://www.gbdinc.org/PDFs/RARE%20EARTH%20PAPER%20FROM%20T.%20STEWART%20JUNE%209%202 011.pdf.

China's Concerns over its Position as the Major Global Supplier of Rare Earths: "Seller's Remorse?"

Overheated rare earth production in China during the 1990s and the early 2000s generated a fragmented industry with thousands of mines, many engaging in reckless mining and illicit production. In order to maximize profits, these small companies often ignored safety and environmental regulations and fiercely competed with each other for export deals. In addition to environmental degradation in China, this overcrowded rare earth sector and often intense competition sharply drove down rare earths prices and, therefore, further pressed producers to cut corners in order to secure their already thinning profit margins. Local governments, which often had vested interests, often tolerated these practices.[34]

In addition to illicit rare earth production, smuggling also became widespread, which exacerbated resource depletion and kept prices low. According to *China Business News,* about 20,000 tons of rare earths were smuggled from China in 2008, which was estimated to have accounted for one-third of the total volume of rare earths leaving China that year.[35] This smuggling is often the main reason behind the discrepancies between the official statistics and the actual data of rare earth production and exports in China.

Chinese policymakers and industry experts have voiced concerns over the perceived rapid depletion of their exhaustible rare earth resources. They contend that the rare earth deposits in China account for less than half of total global reserves; however, the country mines and provides over 95% of the global supply. Rare earth production in China has far outpaced the sustainable level, which makes Chinese officials concerned that such a disproportionately high level of output could soon deplete their resources. The Chinese government is also concerned that overproduction and illegal mining often came at the cost of environmental degradation – safety or environmental protection is often ignored in pursuit of revenue potential.[36]

The Chinese media have repeatedly exposed incidents of water system and farmland contamination in rare earth mining areas, from Inner Mongolia to southern provinces such as Guangdong and Jiangxi.[37] In the southern provinces, rare earths can be found in high concentration in clays and soil a few feet underground. As a result, the 1990s saw an explosion of the number of poorly constructed and maintained local mines that were both polluting and wasteful, leaving behind contaminated soil and water. In November of 2011, during a product quality inspection, China's General Administration of Quality Supervision found that 19 of 85 tea products contained excessive levels of toxic rare earths, including a batch of Lipton tea produced and sold in China by Unilever. Unilever later stated that the rare earth metals had come from the soil where the tea was grown and had nothing to do with its production process.[38]

---

[34] Xinhua, *Outlook Weekly,* Issue No. 201130. http://news.sina.com.cn/c/sd/2011-07-23/195622864615.shtml.

[35] Xinhua, "China mulls plans to curb rare earth smuggling," Sept. 14, 2009. The Chinese Customs' data showed that 39,500 tons of rare earth oxide were exported from China in 2008. http://www.china.org.cn/environment/2009-09/14/content_18523309 htm.

[36] Xinhua, *Outlook Weekly,* Issue No. 201130. http://news.sina.com.cn/c/sd/2011-07-23/195622864615.shtml. Also see *Reuters,* "Fight for Rare Earth," November 2010 http://graphics.thomsonreuters.com/F/11/RareEarths.pdf

[37] Ibid.

[38] *Financial Times,* "Lipton Tea Faces Safety Scandal in China," November 11, 2011; *China Daily,* "Harmful Rare Earth Found in Lipton Tea Samples," November 11, 2011, http://www.chinadaily.com.cn/china/2011-11/11/content_14075815 htm.

China currently argues that it is now moving to consolidate production and put supplies of a critical and exhaustible resource on a more sustainable footing. China maintains that rare earth export prices have been too low to reflect its virtual monopoly position. Moreover, such dominance, in view of the Chinese industry experts and policymakers, should assist China to move up the supply chain and engage in rare earth application and end products, not just being the world's supplier of raw materials.[39] In recent years, China has put in place a series of industry and trade policies, aiming to capitalize on its dominance of rare earth supply.

China's Rare Earth Policy and Implications

The Chinese government has introduced and implemented a series of policies to regulate rare earth production, stabilize prices, and control exports – some policy measures seem to be aimed at more internal control; some have more to do with influencing global supply and prices; while other policies seem to have long term goals which are in line with China's overall industrial policy goal. Chinese export quotas, duties, and license requirements have caused considerable concerns worldwide because these restrictions not only distort global trade of raw materials but also grant Chinese companies easier and cheaper access to rare earths, among other raw materials.

In 2006, China began decreasing rare earth exports, citing internal demand and environmental concerns. This generated supply uncertainties among key industries worldwide such as automotive and electronics and caused significant price increases throughout 2009, 2010, and during the first three quarters of 2011. As a result, industries have been forced to raise prices; some have chosen to relocate to China for cheaper and more reliable supply of rare earths (see a later section of this report).

Production Quotas, Licenses, Resource Tax, and Stockpiles

Since the early 1990s, the Chinese central government has been developing production plans for strategic commodities, including rare earths. China's Ministry of Land and Resources (MLR) issues production quotas to provincial governments, who then assign quotas to individual mining companies under their jurisdictions. Despite the published production quotas, the actual rare earth output (illegal and unlicensed production not included) has been significantly higher than the target.[40]

In 2008 and 2009, the Chinese government started to implement regulations to assert greater control over the rare earth industry. For example, in 2008, the MLR issued *Guidelines for Development of National Mineral Resources 2008-2015,* a government directive with the stated goal of protecting and rationally utilizing China's valuable natural resources for the period 2008 to 2015. This development plan designated rare earths as protected mineral commodities, such as tungsten and antimony. Exploration and production of these protected commodities was to be strictly controlled by the government. The MLR also suspended new applications nationwide for survey or mining licenses for rare earths for an extended period of time.[41]

---

[39] Xinhua, *Outlook Weekly,* Issue No. 201130. http://news.sina.com.cn/c/sd/2011-07-23/195622864615.shtml.

[40] Pui-Kwan Tse, *China's Rare Earth Industry*, U.S. Geological Survey, Open File Report 2011-1042, p.5.

[41] Cindy Hurst, *China's Rare Earth Elements Industry: What Can the West Learn?*; Institute for the Analysis of Global Security (March 2010), p. 22; Testimony by W. David Menzie (U.S. Geological Survey) before the U.S.- China (continued...)

In November 2011, the Chinese government started to levy a higher resource tax on rare earths – increasing the previous rate of RMB 0.4 to 30 yuan per ton to RMB 0.4 to 60 yuan per ton (approximately up to US $ 9.50), depending on the type of rare earths.[42]

The central government reportedly has been building strategic reserves of rare earth metals, among other commodities deemed strategic. Such efforts could give China more power to regulate supply-demand relationships and influence global rare earth prices and supplies. According to a *Wall Street Journal* report, the recent Chinese rare earths stockpiling, under the direction of the MLR, began with a pilot project in 2010 at Baotou Steel Rare Earth Hi-Tech Co. in Inner Mongolia. At least 10 storage facilities are being constructed, where stockpiles may eventually reach 100,000 metric tons.[43]

In February 2011, the MLR announced plans to establish national rare earth regions. The first one will be in Ganzhou, Jiangxi Province, an area with significant medium-heavy rare earth deposits. The central or provincial government will plan and direct the exploration and mining activities.[44]

Industry Restructuring and Consolidation

The Chinese central government has long envisioned a highly consolidated domestic rare earth industry controlled by a few large state-owned firms, which would enable the government to take control of the sector, specifically, to rein in "oversupply" in the global market and stop price wars among the smaller suppliers in China. Over the years the government has been directing industry consolidation by shutting down smaller, illegal operations and merging bigger producers.

Industry Consolidation

The general goal, as stated in "Plans for Developing the Rare Earth Industry 2009-2015," is to establish three large rare earth production districts and two production systems nationwide. The plan will divide the industry into three districts: North (Inner Mongolia and Shandong), South (mainly Jiangxi, Guangdong, Fujian, Hunan, and Guangxi), and West (Sichuan). The two rare earth systems involve light rare earths in northern China and medium-to-heavy rare earths in southern China,[45] as illustrated in **Figure 7**.

(...continued)

Economic and Security Review Commission Hearing on "China's Global Quest for Resources and Implications for the United States," January 26, 2012.

[42] *The Wall Street Journal*, "China Expands Resource Tax to Nation," October 10, 2011. The Renminbi (RMB) is the official name of China's currency and the yuan is the primary unit of the RMB.

[43] *The Wall Street Journal*, "Tightening Its Grip, China Begins to Stockpile Rare-Earth Metals," February 7, 2011.

[44] The central Chinese government website, http://www.gov.cn/jrzg/2011-02/10/content_1801188.htm, as viewed on January 31, 2012.

[45] Xinhua, *Oriental Outlook,* Issue No. 2011007. http://news.sina.com.cn/c/sd/2011-02-21/11421988124.shtml. CRS used the original Chinese-language version of the report.; Cindy Hurst, *China's Rare Earth Elements Industry: What Can the West Learn?* Institute for the Analysis of Global Security (March 2010), p. 22.

Figure 7. Planned Rare Earth Production Districts in China

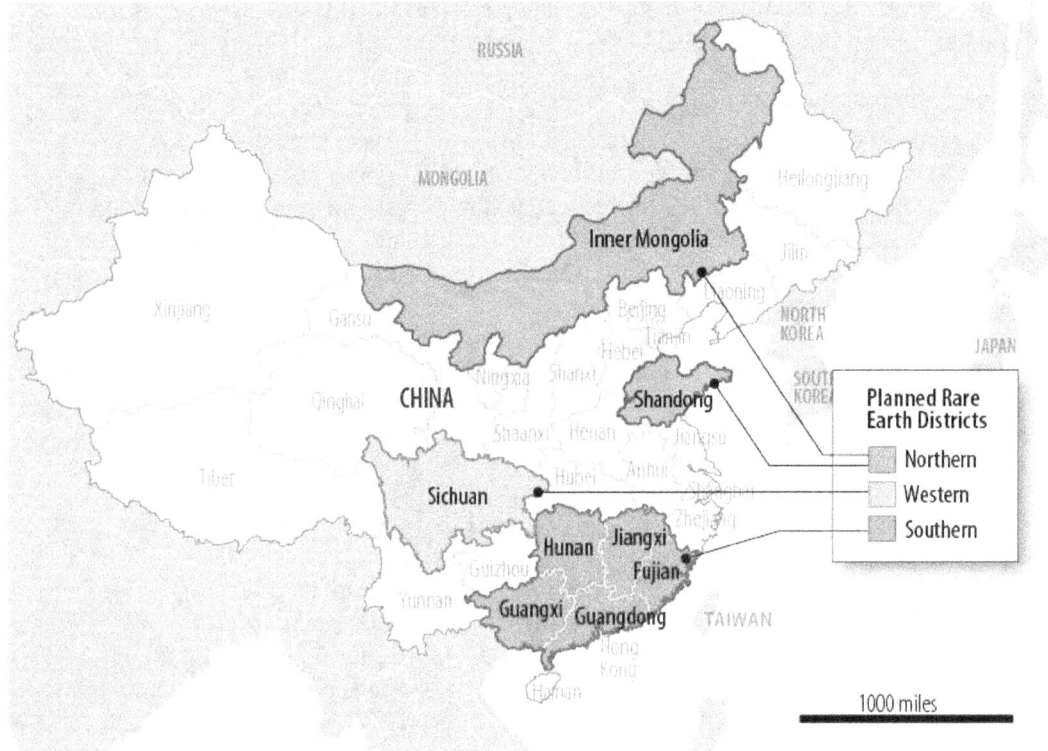

Source: Plans for Developing the Rare Earth Industry 2009-2015.

Note: Map prepared by Congressional Research Service (CRS).

As early as 2002, the State Council approved a proposal to establish two major rare earths groups nationwide: one in the north and one in the south. The ultimate goal, reportedly, is to create a unified front for the entire Chinese rare earth industry – unified production, purchasing, pricing, and sales.[46] However, since it has been difficult to balance or negotiate the interests among business enterprises and stakeholders, this vision has yet to come to fruition.

Results Vary

In northern China, where the industry tends to be more concentrated than the southern part of the country, Baotou Steel Rare Earth High-Tech Co. (Baotou Rare Earth) has been chosen as the forerunner in industry consolidation. The Inner Mongolia government issued a directive in May 2011, and announced Baotou Steel Rare Earth High-Tech Co. to be the single government-controlled monopoly to mine and process ore in northern China. The government also listed the names of 35 other companies, ordering 31 mostly private rare earth companies to close and 4 other companies to merge into Baotou Rare Earth.[47]

The more fragmented southern market, however, has several big companies competing for dominance. With anticipation that rare earth prices will go up, local governments and

---

[46] Xinhua, *Outlook Weekly,* Issue No. 201130. http://news.sina.com.cn/c/sd/2011-07-23/195622864615.shtml.

[47] Ibid; *The New York Times,* "China consolidates grip on rare earths" (September 15, 2011).

stakeholders may resist consolidation and seek to protect local mineral deposits. For example, state-owned companies such as China Minmetals Corp. and Aluminum Corporation of China (Chinalco) have been pushing to enter the market of Jiangxi Province (rich in heavy rare earth deposits, especially in Ganzhou), only to find out that the local Ganzhou Rare Earth Minerals Industry Co. Ltd. has a monopoly over the resources. [48]

The government plans to consolidate rare earth industry in southern China and let three companies control 80% of the production there within the next several years. All three, reportedly, are former government ministries that were spun out as corporations, with the central government still holding major stakes. [49]

It remains to be seen how fast and to what extent these policy measures will bring results as planned. In 2012, a year of transition in China's top leadership, how to balance central and local interests may take priority. In addition, economic growth, employment, and social stability concerns also weigh heavily in the minds of policymakers.

However, if these proposed four state-owned companies – Baotou in the north and the three companies in southern region – were to control China's rare earths industry, they may limit sales or impose other restrictions to foreign buyers, a "business" tactic that some maintain may not be easy to challenge.

New Industry Guidelines

In May 2011, the Chinese State Council issued "Guidelines to Promote Sustainable and Sound Development of the Rare Earth Industry." The government reiterated its commitment to keep rare earth mining under control by keeping the existing export quota system, suspending issuance of new production licenses, and cracking down on illegal mining and rare earths smuggling. [50]

The government's focus seems to be on consolidating the industry and optimizing its structure, by drastically reducing the number of rare earth miners and smelters, phasing out outdated and polluting mining practices, and encouraging companies to upgrade their technologies. [51]

China's Rare Earth Export Regime

Export Tax Rebates

In the 1990s, the government encouraged companies to export rare earth products by granting rebates on export taxes paid by domestic producers. In 2000, in order to meet increasing domestic demand, the Chinese government reduced export rebates for a number of commodities deemed

---

[48] Open Source Center, "Beijing Review: 'Rare Power'" (June 7, 2011). https://www.opensource.gov/portal/server.pt/gateway/PTARGS_0_0_200_203_121123_43/content/Display/CPP20110 610707006.

[49] Ibid.

[50] Ibid; The central PRC government website, http://www.gov.cn/banshi/2011-08/09/content_1922128.htm, as viewed on January 31, 2012.

[51] Ibid.

"strategic," including rare earths. In 2005, rare earth export rebates were abolished to curb rare earth exports, and trade of rare earth concentrate was banned.[52]

Export Licenses

Foreign companies are prohibited from mining rare earths in China. They are also restricted from participating in rare earth smelting and separation projects, unless they form joint ventures with Chinese partners. Like their Chinese counterparts, Sino-foreign joint ventures are permitted to export their products under a licensing system managed by the Ministry of Commerce (MOC).[53]

The Chinese government has gradually reduced the number of licensed companies in recent years through tightening licensing rules and environmental regulations. In 2006, 47 Chinese domestic and 12 joint-venture rare earth companies received export licenses. In 2009, there were 23 domestic and 11 joint-venture licensees. These numbers were further reduced to 22 domestic and 10 joint-venture license holders in 2010 and, to 22 domestic and 9 joint ventures companies in 2011.[54]

For 2012, the central government has allocated first-round export quotas to 9 companies, with 17 other companies awaiting inspection results.[55] If these 17 companies meet environmental standards, the total count of companies with export permits would be 26, which would be lower than in 2011. No specific information is available about the breakdown of domestic and joint-venture companies for 2012.

Export Duties

In 2007, the Chinese government started to levy export duties to manage and control the variety and quantity of rare earth products to be shipped out of China. Initially, the duty rates were set at 10% and applied to fewer items than today.[56]

The duty rates have increased over the years and now range from 15% - 25%. They are applied to more rare earth products. For example, China added a separate category in its 2011 export duty schedule for ferroalloys containing more than 10% of rare earth elements, and subjected them to a 25% export duty.[57]

---

[52] Pui-Kwan Tse, *China's Rare Earth Industry*, U.S. Geological Survey, Open File Report 2011-1042, p.6. Rare earth ore is ground into fine particles, which are then concentrated using separation techniques such as froth flotation, magnetic separation, and gravity or electrostatic concentration. Rare earth concentrate contains a higher grade/concentration of rare earth than the raw ore but is still in the form of the original natural minerals.

[53] Ibid.

[54] Ibid.

[55] Bloomberg.com, "China 2012 Rare-Earth Export Quota Unchanged as Sales Slump," December 28, 2011.

[56] Pui-Kwan Tse, *China's Rare Earth Industry*, U.S. Geological Survey, Open File Report 2011-1042, p.8.

[57] Stewart, Drake, Dwyer, and Gong, Rare Earths, An Update, A Fresh Look at the Supplier(s), the Buyers, and the Trade Rules, p. 7. Ferroalloys are alloys of iron and one or more other elements, such as manganese, silicon, and rare earths.

Export Quotas

In addition to export duties and licenses, China also applies quotas to limit the quantity of rare earths that can be exported. These annual quotas are allocated to domestic firms and joint-ventures with foreign investors. Between 2005 and 2010, the total quotas have been reduced almost every year as the domestic demand for rare earths has considerably increased. Joint ventures with foreign investment have seen their allocated quotas cut more sharply than their domestic Chinese counterparts, especially in 2010 (see **Table 1**).

The official 2011 rare earths export quota was established comparable to the 2010 level. However, in 2011, only half of the 2011 export quota was filled due to sluggish global demand and the decreasing rare earths prices during the second half of 2011.

Table 1. China's Export Quotas on Rare Earths

(metric tons)

	2005	**2006**	**2007**	**2008**	**2009**	**2010**	**2011**	**2012**
Domestic	48,010	45,000	43,574	34,156	31,310	22,513	22,712	N/A
Joint Venture	17,570	16,070	16,069	15,834	16,845	7,746	7,472	N/A
Total	65,580	61,070	59,643	49,990	48,155	30,259	30,184	31,130

Sources: China Rare Earth website (http://www.cre.net/show.php?contentid=97130, as viewed on February 28, 2012): 2009-2011 Rare Earth Export Quotas; Pui-Kwan Tse, *China's Rare Earth Industry*, U.S. Geological Survey, Open File Report 2011-1042, Table 1.

Notes: China's Ministry of Commerce announced that the first-round quota figures of 24,904 tons represents 80% of the 2012 full year quota. The full-year quota is calculated based on the MOC announcement.

Another contributing factor is that, amid complaints over China's control of rare earth supply, many manufacturers sought to reduce rare earth usage and/or seek alternative materials, in order to contain costs and reduce dependence on Chinese supply. For example, Toyota Motor Corp., reportedly, is working to develop a new electric motor for hybrids cars that eliminates the use of rare earth magnets used in the motors. The new motor Toyota is developing would exploit the common and inexpensive induction motor, which use electromagnets – magnets that only have their magnetic attraction when power is applied to them.[58] In August 2011, General Electric (GE) announced the development of wind turbine generators that would reduce dependence on rare earths, seeking to change the current situation in which offshore wind turbines may contain as much as half a ton of rare earth metals. W.R. Grace & Co., reportedly, began selling an oil-refining catalyst with reduced usage of rare earths.[59]

The 2012 Quota System

China announced that it would keep its 2012 rare earth export quotas virtually unchanged, leaving them higher than expected. However, considering the fact that only half of the quotas were utilized in the previous year, this does not necessarily suggest that the government is loosening its

---

[58] *The Wall Street Journal*, "Toyota Tries to Break Reliance on China," January 14, 2011.

[59] Bloomberg.com, "Rare Earths Fall as Toyota Develops Alternatives: Commodities," September 28, 2011.

control over rare earths exports. Several significant changes to the 2012 quota system suggest the government has become more specific and stricter in its effort to conserve resources and protect the environment.

The Chinese government allocated 10,546 tons of the first-round of export quotas to 9 companies that have met the government's environmental protection standards. Another 14,358 tons were reserved and would be granted to 17 other companies if they meet the standards by the end of July 2012.[60]

For the first time, quotas assigned to qualified companies, specifically, were further split into two groups—light and medium-heavy rare earths. Separate export quotas were set for each group. According to the first-round quota announced, light rare earths account for over 87% of the total volume.[61]

"Technology for Resources"

Not permitted by the Chinese government to have mining operations, foreign companies may not participate in rare earth smelting and separation without a domestic partner. However, they are encouraged to invest in downstream rare earth processing in China and development of new applications and products.

In 2002, the National Development and Reform Commission (NDRC) issued a directive, "(Temporary) Regulations of Foreign Investments in the Rare Earth Sector,"[62] which provides that :

- Foreign companies are prohibited from any rare earth mining business;

- Foreign companies are not permitted to participate in rare earth smelting and separation projects by themselves. Exceptions will be made when they form joint ventures with Chinese partners.

- Foreign companies are encouraged to invest in downstream rare earth processing in China and development of new rare earth applications and products.

Many analysts contend that China's policies on rare earth exports reflect an attempt by Beijing to induce foreign companies that use rare earths to move production facilities to China and to transfer technology to Chinese partners, in exchange for a stable, reliable, and relatively low-cost supply of rare earths. For example, according to a Japanese publication, the *Daily Yomiuri*, Japanese business representatives have been told by Chinese government officials that, in exchange for a stable supply of rare earths, Japanese manufacturers using rare earths should move their plants to China.[63]

---

[60] Bloomberg.com, "China 2012 Rare-Earth Export Quota Unchanged as Sales Slump," December 28, 2011; China Rare Earth website (http://www.cre net/show.php?contentid=100015): 2012 1st round rare earth quota higher than market expectation, with distinction between light and heavy rare earths, December 28, 2011, as viewed on January 31, 2012. CRS used the original Chinese-language version of the announcement.

[61] Ibid.

[62] NDRC website: http://www.ndrc.gov.cn/wzly/zcfg/wzzczjtc/t20050715_36904 htm, as viewed on February 1, 2012. The document is in Chinese.

[63] *Daily Yomiuri Online,* "Stable Rare Earth Supply Sought," September 8, 2011.

A high-level delegation of Japanese business leaders visiting China in September 2011 was reportedly told by Chinese Vice Premier Li Keqiang that China expected technical cooperation with Japan relating to rare earth industries, noting "Japan possesses excellent technology related to the exploration and use of rare earths."[64] Media reports have presented some evidence that some Japanese firms may be responding to some of these pressures. For example:

- Hitachi Metals, a major producer of high-powered magnets, reportedly indicated in August 2011, that it was contemplating moving production of some of its neodymium-based magnets to China.[65]

- In September 2011, Toyota announced that it was planning to manufacture components (such as electric motors and batteries) for its hybrid cars in China, a move that some analysts speculated was motivated, in part, by Toyota's desire to gain access to rare earths.[66]

This "technology for resources" strategy[67] fits well with the government's goal of expanding its rare earth industry to the more sophisticated processing sectors. Many of these measures appear to be part of a broader set of industrial policies China has put forth in an effort to become a global leader in innovation and high technology (see **Text Box**). Some local governments offer incentives to persuade foreign companies to move factories to China because they believe foreign involvement would bring resource-rich regions a chance to become high-tech centers.

China's Industrial Policies on Rare Earths

In 2006 China's State Council released "the National Medium-and Long-Term Program for Science and Technology Development (2006-2020)," which set out an ambitious plan to modernize the structure of China's economy by transforming it from a global center of low-tech manufacturing to one that is a major center of innovation by the year 2020 and a global innovation leader by 2050. It also seeks to sharply reduce the country's dependence on foreign technology. Developing technologies for manufacturing rare earths was identified as a priority area under the plan. The plan also identifies a number of renewable energy industries which use rare earth materials as well as clean vehicles. These priorities were also listed under China's 12th Five Year Plan (2011-2015), which identified new materials (which includes rare earths), new energy industry, and new energy cars (including electric and hybrid vehicles) among seven "strategic industries" identified for development.

In recent years, China has pursued trade and industrial policies to capitalize on its near monopoly supply of rare earths. The problem, in the view of Chinese policymakers, was that export prices have been too low to reflect their monopoly position and limited supply of such minerals and that their industry occupied the lowest position on the supply chain of rare earth usage. A major priority for China has been to move up the high-technology ladder and foster growth of renewable energy companies. Beijing has promoted the production and domestic use of hybrid cars, wind turbines, solar panels, and biofuels, among others. From 2007 to 2010, China was estimated to have spent $120 billion to $160 billion on renewable energy projects.[68]

---

[64] Ibid.

[65] "Analysis: Japanese Rare Earth Consumers Set Up Shop in China," *Reuters*, August 12, 2011.

[66] BBC, "Toyota to Make hybrid Car Parts in China to Boost Sales," September 5, 2011.

[67] *The Wall Street Journal*, "China Dangles Resources to Investors," August 16, 2010. A senior official with China's Ministry of Industry & Information is reported to have said that, while China had used a "technology for market" strategy before, now they have the expression "technology for resources."

[68] EC Harris, Energy & Manufacturing, *Research Shows the UK Lags Behind in the Global Race For Energy Investment*, Autumn 2010.

In 2010, about 50 foreign companies were already operating in the Baotou Rare Earth Hi-Tech Zone in Inner Mongolia, including France's Rhodia SA. It was reported that the Korea Development Bank had signed a cooperative agreement with Baotou Rare Earth High-Tech Zone to encourage Korean automobile and electronics companies to establish processing factories alone or with Chinese partners.[69]

China's "technology for resources" strategy, backed by a restrictive export regime, has caused concerns around the globe. To foreign companies, it seems the Chinese government is using rare earth resources to attract foreign investment that could bring in sophisticated technologies that Chinese companies need to advance to the more value-added rare earth processing and application sectors, eventually becoming direct competitors.

In addition, non-Chinese manufacturers are widely concerned about the risk of unintended technology transfer and intellectual property infringement. For example, Intematix, a Fremont, California-based company, takes elaborate precautions in this regard. Intematix makes rare earth-based phosphors used in liquid-crystal displays and LED lighting. Reportedly, when Intematix hired Chinese scientists to perfect the production processes in its new factory in China, only three of the scientists had knowledge of the complete chemical formulas.[70]

China's Quest for Rare Earth Resources

With the central government's encouragement and approval, China's major state-owned companies have been actively seeking to secure supplies of raw materials domestically and overseas. The world has seen an increase in these activities since the global recession took place in late 2008, which has weakened demand and kept the investment prices more reasonable. Another important factor is that many mining companies and resources-rich regions are looking for financial investments in a tightened credit market.

This wave of "going global" from China includes energy projects and mining assets, including rare earth resources outside China. Two key examples are the acquisition bids by Chinese companies for Molycorp of the United States and Lynas of Australia, the two rare earths mines now positioned to provide significant amount of rare earths outside of China.

Molycorp

In 2005, China National Offshore Oil Corp. (CNOOC), a state-owned enterprise, put forward a $18.5 billion acquisition bid to acquire the American oil and gas company, Unocal Corporation (UCL). Molycorp, whose Mountain Pass rare earth mine had been shut down in 2002, was then a unit of Unocal. Facing strong opposition from U.S. political leaders who voiced deep concerns over transfer of U.S. oil reserves to a company controlled by the Chinese government, CNOOC eventually dropped the bid.[71]

---

[69] Ibid.

[70] Ibid; Intematix company website: http://www.intematix.com/company, as viewed on February 3, 2012.

[71] *Business Week*, "Why China's Unocal Bid Ran out of Gas," August 4, 2005;

Business analysts seemed to agree that CNOOC was interested in Unocal's assets in Southeast Asia.[72] It is not clear whether the rare earth resource at Mountain Pass was one of the congressional concerns at that time. According to the testimony by Jeffery A. Green at a hearing before the U.S.- China Economic And Security Review Commission: " … little attention was paid on Capitol Hill or within the Executive Branch to the inclusion or implications of the sale of the rare earth resource." [73]

Chevron subsequently bought Unocal in 2005, acquiring Molycorp and the Mountain Pass mine as part of the acquisition. In 2008, privately-held Molycorp Minerals LLC acquired the Mountain Pass facility from Chevron, which has been developing rare earth processing technologies and products. In 2009, Molycorp began processing stockpiled bastnasite concentrate. In 2011, Molycorp, which had become a publicly traded company, started the mining of fresh bastnasite ore at Mountain Pass.[74]

In March 2012, Molycorp announced that it planned to acquire Neo Material Technologies, a major rare earths processing company listed in Toronto. Neo has plants in China and Thailand and, reportedly, earns 64% of its 2011 revenues serving markets in China and Japan.[75] Molycorp plans to begin exports of rare earths to China to be processed into magnetic materials (see **Text Box**).

However, some industry officials and policymakers have expressed concerns that the deal could reinforce China's dominance in rare earth production and processing and may do little to help the United States develop its crucial rare earth processing capability. Some are also concerned that rare earths shipped from the United States to China would be subject to Chinese export restrictions once they are processed and ready to leave China.[76]

Molycorp Plans to Buy Major Rare Earth Processor

In March 2012, Molycorp announced plans to acquire Toronto-listed Neo Material Technologies Inc. (Neo), one of the world's leading rare earths processing companies. The proposed deal paves the way for Molycorp to ship rare earth minerals from its California mine to the Chinese operations of a Neo arm called Magnequench to be processed into magnets. Molycorp asserts that the acquisition would give it significant new technological capability and, at the same time, lower production costs as it restarts the Mountain Pass mine.

Magnequench, formerly a GM subsidiary, was a specialized producer of magnet materials based in the United States. In 1995, GM sold Magnequench to a group of investors including state-owned China National Non-Ferrous Metals Import & Export Corp. The investment group then opened a plant in China and closed an Indiana plant.

Given the historical and political implications of the deal, industry officials and policymakers are concerned that it could reinforce China's virtual monopoly.

Source: *The Wall Street Journal*, "Rare-Earth Deal Rings China Alarm," March 12, 2012.

---

[72] Ibid.

[73] Testimony by Jeffery A. Green before the U.S.- China Economic And Security Review Commission Hearing on "China's Global Quest for Resources and Implications for the United States" on January 26, 2012.

[74] Molycorp company website: http://www.molycorp.com/AboutUs/OurHistory.aspx, as viewed on February 3, 2012.

[75] *Financial Times*, "Molycorp to start China rare earth exports after Neo deal" (March 10, 2012); *The Wall Street Journal*, "Rare-earth deal rings China alarm" (March 12, 2012).

[76] Ibid; *The Wall Street Journal*, "Deal Shows China's Sway in Rare-Earth Minerals," March 11, 2012.

Lynas

In May 2009, a less publicized event occurred when China Non-Ferrous Metal Mining (Group) Co. (CNMC) attempted to acquire a major stake in Lynas Corporation of Australia. In return, CNMC would secure full funding for development of Lynas' Mt. Weld mine in Western Australia, the world's largest single-deposit rare earths mine. However, after extended review of the deal by the Australian government, its Foreign Investment Review Board (FIRB) requested a number of changes. In particular, FIRB requested that the proposed ownership to be held by CNMC be less than 50% and, the number of Board Director positions be held by CNMC to be less than half of the Board. CNMC rescinded its offer.[77]

Rare Earth Trade Issues

China has increasingly used a number of export restrictions (including export taxes, quotas, licenses, and prohibitions) on a wide range of products, particularly raw materials.[78] According to the United States Geological Survey (USGS), China is a major global producer and, in some cases, a dominant producer of many raw and processed materials. For example, in 2010, China accounted for more than 80% of global production of antimony, magnesium metal, rare earths, and tungsten. It also accounted for between 50% and 80% of global production of over a dozen other materials.[79] China was the largest global producer of 37 out of the 80 mineral commodities tracked by the USGS.[80]

A 2010 WTO review of China's trade policies states, "export restrictions, explicit or implicit, are a major feature of China's trade regime." For example, in 2009, China's trade regime applied export quotas to 173 tariff lines,[81] export licensing requirements to 231 lines, and export taxes to 353 tariff lines (258 of which were interim taxes).[82] The WTO review stated:

> Whether intended or not, export restraints for whatever reason tend to reduce export volumes of the targeted products and divert supplies to the domestic market, leading to a downward pressure on the domestic prices of these products. The resulting gap between domestic prices and world prices constitutes implicit assistance to domestic downstream processors of the targeted products and thus provides them a competitive advantage. Insofar as China is a

---

[77] Lynas Corporation Ltd. Annual Report 2009, p.53.
http://www.lynascorp.com/content/upload/files/Reports/Annual_Report_2009_778195.pdf.

[78] According to the WTO, raw materials affected by Chinese restraints include sawn timber, coke, oil, rare earth, antimony and its products, tungsten and its products, zinc ore, tin and its products, silver, indium, molybdenum, phosphate rocks, carbide, fluorspar, talc, magnesium, and bauxite. China also imposes export restraints on a number of agricultural products.

[79] Statement of W. David Menzie, Chief of Global Minerals Analysis, National Minerals Information Center, U.S. Geological Survey, before the U.S.-China Economic and Security Review Commission hearing on "China's Global Quest for Resources and Implications for the United States," January 26, 2012. These materials are bismuth, germanium, indium, pig iron, mercury, silicon, fused alumina, barite, cement, fluorspar, natural graphite, lime, magnesium compounds, wollastonite, and natural zeolites.

[80] Ibid.

[81] These tariff lines refer to those listed in China's tariff schedule, based on the Harmonized Tariff System on an 8-digit level.

[82] WTO, *Trade Policy Review, China*, June 2010, p.44.

major supplier of such a product, export restraints may also shift the terms of trade in China's favour.[83]

Prices for Chinese Rare Earth

As noted earlier in **Figure 6,** the quantity of China's rare earth exports have been declining since 2003. From 2003 to about 2009, that decline did not appear to have much of an effect on the price of China's rare earth exports. However, efforts by the Chinese government in 2010 to further tighten its control over the production and export of rare earths appear to have created global shortages of many types of rare earths and sharply raised prices. For example, in July 2010, China announced that it would reduce its export quota of rare earth elements by 70% during the second half of 2010 over the previous year's level (or a 40% drop for the full year over 2009 levels). In addition, the Chinese government in 2011 reportedly imposed minimum price levels for rare earth exports. Such factors sharply reduced foreign demand for Chinese rare earths so that China's 2011 export quota level was not reached.[84] According to Lynas Corporation, 2011 saw an "extraordinary explosion in rare earths prices" and that such price rises "reached unsustainable levels for industry."[85]

As indicated in **Figure 8**, the average price of U.S. rare earth imports from China (based on the U.S. customs value per metric ton) rose from $5,589 in January 2010 to $53,024 in January 2011 (nearly a 10-fold increase), and by September 2011, rare earth prices surged to $158,389. From January 2010 to September 2011, the average price of imported rare earths from China surged by 2,734%. Average prices for imported Chinese rare earths have dropped sharply since September 2011, falling to $46,694 per metric ton in February 2012, a 70.5% decline. However, prices on U.S. imported rare earths from China in February 2012 were nearly 11 times higher than they were in February 2010. Some analysts contend that the drop in Chinese rare earth prices after September 2011 resulted from a sharp drop in foreign demand. This was likely caused by several factors, including the movement of some foreign manufacturing that use rare earths to China, the drawing down of rare earth inventories, switching to alternative materials, and possibly curtailing production to avoid paying the extremely high prices.[86]

---

[83] Ibid.

[84] These are discussed in more detail in a later section titled "Chinese Rare Earths Export Regime."

[85] Lynas Corporation, Lynas Annual General Meeting 2011 Chairman Address.

[86] *The New York Times*, "Prices of Rare Earth Metals Declining Sharply," November 16, 2011.

Figure 8. Monthly Customs Value per Metric Ton of U.S. Rare Earth Imports from China: January 2010 - February 2012

($)

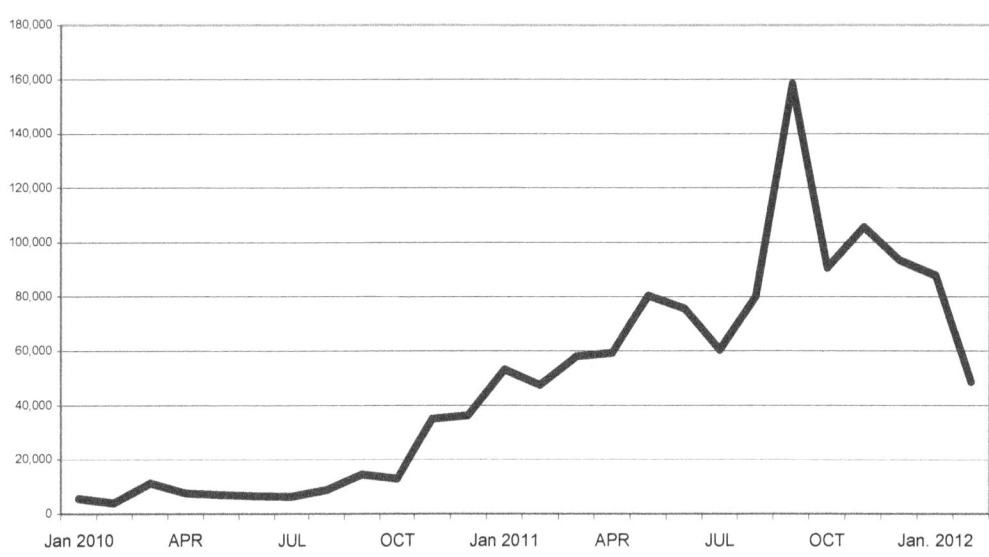

Source: USITC Dataweb.

Note: Rare earth categories as defined by the U.S. Geological Survey. Data indicate average prices for rare earth imports. Prices for individual rare earths differ markedly.

Impact of China's Rare Earth Policies on U.S. Firms

According to the U.S. Geological Survey, the estimated distribution of rare earths by end use in the United States as a percent of total usage in 2011 was as follows: catalysts, which are largely used in oil refining and autos (47%); metallurgical applications and alloys (13%); alloys, (11%); glass polishing and ceramics (10%); permanent magnets (9%); ceramics (5%); and rare-earth phosphors for computer monitors, lighting, radar, televisions, and x-ray-intensifying film (5%).[87]

Media reports have cited a number of U.S. firms that have raised concerns over how high-priced rare earth imports from China are affecting their production costs and business decisions:

- In July 2011, General Electric issued a statement on rare earths, saying that: "Rare earths are undergoing extreme cost increases due to unprecedented market forces. In less than 12 months, costs of some rare earth oxide materials used in lighting products have experienced increases ranging from 500% to more than 2,000%, and they continue to climb. For perspective, if the rate of inflation on the rare earth element europium oxide were applied to a $2.00 cup of coffee, the new cost would be $24.55."[88]

---

[87] U.S. Geological Survey, *Mineral Commodity Summaries*, January 2012, p. 128.

[88] GE, *Rare Earth FAQs*, July 17, 2011.

- In August 2011, Intematix, a U.S. company that produces phosphor, stated that, in response to rare earth shortages, it was moving some of its manufacturing to China while developing alternative phosphors in the United States.[89] An article in the New York Times stated that the company would have preferred to build its new factory near its headquarters in Fremont, California.[90]

- In September 2011, Michael N. Silver, chairman and chief executive of American Elements, a U.S. chemical company, was quoted as saying that the "high cost of rare earths is having a significant chilling effect on wind turbine and electric motor production in spite of offsetting government subsidies for green tech products."[91]

- In September 2011, John Galyen, president of Danfoss North America (a manufacturer of energy-efficient pumps and valves that depend on rare earth magnets) testified before a congressional committee that, "My over-arching point is this. China's rare earth elements' strategy is an issue affecting the U.S. and friendly country industries broadly. It is threatening our leadership in such innovative technologies and our ability for our country to meet energy-saving goals. And it appears that their strategy will also attract high technology manufacturing, investment, and jobs to China while offering local supply and price advantage."[92]

- In October 2011, Peter Dent, Vice President of Business Development, Electron Energy Corporation, in testimony before the United States Trade Representative (USTR), stated: "Practically, the aftermath of the quota reductions last year resulted in skyrocketing prices, long and uncertain deliveries, very fast payment terms with advance payments and fundamental questions about whether or not materials would be available at all at any price...Customers of products containing rare earths have been working to redesign systems using less rare earths, opting for lesser performing substitutes. This money would have better been deployed on capital equipment, adding employees, workforce training and facilities expansion to enhance international competitiveness, but instead it sits in drums full of rare earth inventories and lost time and effort." In addition, Dent stated that the huge price gap between Chinese rare earths consumed domestically and Chinese rare earth exports "puts Chinese industrial users of rare earths at a substantial structural competitive advantage over their competitors in the rest of the world." Dent went on to warn that the transfer of production by foreign technology companies to China in order to gain access to rare earths involved "serious risk of unintended technology transfer to China, which would constitute an irreversible loss of intellectual property."[93]

---

[89] According to a company official: "By manufacturing our aluminates and garnet phosphors in China, we can buy our rare earth materials there instead of having to export them. "In the U.S., we are making our nitride and silicate phosphors which use only very small quantities of rare earths." Source: EE Times, "Rare Earths Get Rarer, August 8, 2011.

[90] *The New York Times*, "Chasing Rare Earths, Foreign Companies Expand in China," August 24, 2011.

[91] *The New York Times*, "China Consolidates Grip on Rare Earths," September 15, 2011.

[92] Testimony by John Galyen, president of Danfoss North America, before the House Committee on Foreign Affairs, Subcommittee on Asia and the Pacific, *Hearing on China's Monopoly on Rare Earths: Implications for U.S. Foreign and Security Policy*, September 21, 2011.

[93] USTR, "China's Compliance with WTO Commitments," Testimony by Peter Dent, Vice President, Business (continued...)

- A study by Bloomberg Government attempted to evaluate the effects the rising costs of rare earths had on two major producers of hard disk drives: Seagate Technologies Plc and Western Digital Corp. The report estimated that the rising costs of rare earth from July 2011 to September 2011 reduced the net income of Seagate and Western Digital by 37% and 21%, respectively.[94]

Implications for Chinese Firms

Some analysts contend that China's recent efforts to tighten its rare earth export restrictions may be, in part, intended to ensure that its own domestic firms that use rare earths have adequate access to such resources because global demand for rare earths may have already overtaken global supply (see **Figure 9**). Some analysts predict that China's production of rare earths may soon be unable to meet its growing domestic demand, which may prompt the Chinese government to further limit rare earth exports and/or to seek to obtain rare earths from abroad.[95] According to the USGS, China's consumption of its estimated rare earth production has risen from 26.2% in 2000 to 64.2% in 2010.[96]

Figure 9. Chinese and Global Supply and Demand for Rare Earths

(actual and projections through 2015)

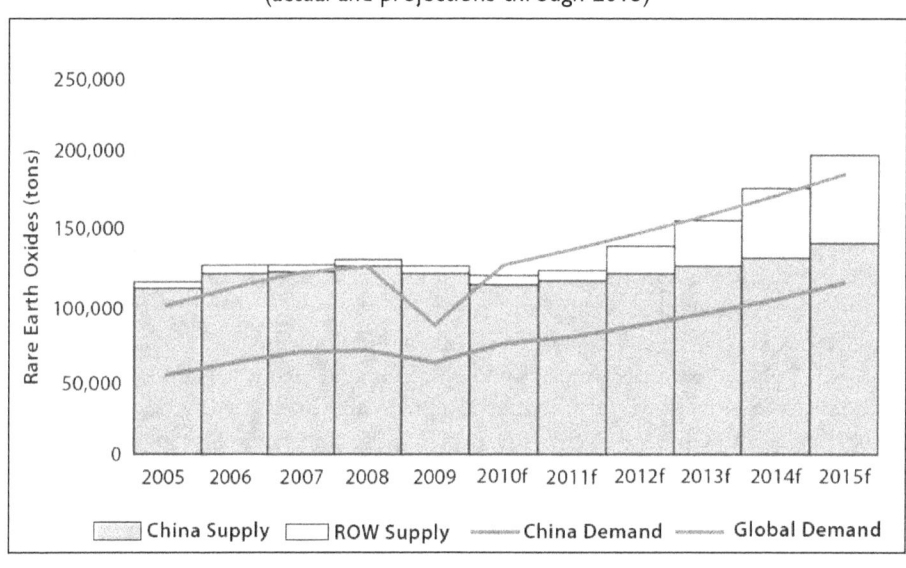

Source: Industrial Minerals Company of Australia (IMCOA), "Meeting the Challenges of Supply this Decade" (March 2011). Note: ROW is the rest of the world.

(...continued)

Development, Electron Energy Corporation, October 5, 2011.

[94] Bloomberg Government, *China's Rare-Earth Policies Erode Technology Profits*, February 3, 2012.

[95] Ernest & Young, *Rare Earth Elements: Opportunities and Challenges*, September 2010. Note, technically, in a free market, when demand is growing faster than supply, the price for that commodity will increase, which could potentially force some Chinese users of rare earths out of the market.

[96] U.S. Geological Survey, *China's Rare-Earth Industry*, Open File Report 2011–1042, 2011, p. 4.

China's export quotas, minimum export prices, and export duties appear to have caused prices of Chinese rare earth exports to become significantly higher than for domestic users in China. For example, according to Lynas Corporation LTD, an Australian rare earth mining company, average prices for eight types of rare earth oxides in the 4th quarter of 2011 were between 70.5% and 557% higher than those for domestic users (see **Table 2**).

Table 2. Average Chinese Domestic and Export Prices for Selected Rare Earth Oxides: 4th Quarter 2011

Rare Earth Oxide	Chinese Domestic Prices ($ per kg)	Chinese Export Prices ($ per kg)	Percent Difference Between Chinese Export Prices and Chinese Domestic Prices
Lanthanum Oxide	18.3	66.5	263.4%
Cerium Oxide	20.7	59.3	186.5%
Neodymium Oxide	122.8	244.2	98.9%
Praseodymium Oxide	107.0	209.6	95.9%
Samarium Oxide	14.5	95.3	557.2%
Dysprosium Oxide	1,085.4	2,032.1	87.2%
Europium Oxide	2,228.4	3,800.0	70.5%
Terbium Oxide	1,765.1	2,973.9	68.5%

Source: Lynas Corporation LTD at http://www.lynascorp.com/index.asp.

The U.S. Response to China's Export Restrictions on Rare Earths

China's increased use of export restraints and other discriminatory measures on rare earths has led stakeholders (especially in the United States, Japan, and EU) to call for trade action against China. One of the first efforts in the United States to address China's rare earth policies occurred in September 2010.

Chinese restrictions on rare earths were included in a Section 301petition (dealing with unfair trade practices) that was filed in September 2010 with the USTR by the United Steel, Paper and Forestry, Rubber, Manufacturing, Energy, Allied Industrial and Service Workers International Union, AFL-CIO CLC (USW). The petition sought to address a number of China's policies and practices affecting trade and investment in green technologies.[97] The main export restrictions on rare earths identified by the USW petition included export duties, quotas, and licensing procedures. The USW stated that "China's reliance on WTO-inconsistent export restraints to dominate the world market in rare earth and other minerals not only nullifies and impairs benefits

---

[97] In addition to China's restrictions on rare earths, the petition alleged export restraints on tungsten and antimony, subsidies contingent on export performance or on the use of domestic over imported goods, discrimination against foreign companies and goods, technology transfer requirements on foreign investment in China, and domestic subsidy programs.

accruing to the United States under the WTO Agreement, it fundamentally distorts trade and competition in the green technology sector, among others."[98]

The USTR decided to narrow its investigation to include only Chinese grants (subsidies) given to domestic wind turbine manufacturers that agreed to use key parts and components made in China rather than purchasing imports, and in December 2010, it brought a WTO dispute resolution case against China.[99] In February 2011, China agreed to remove the discriminatory subsidies.[100]

The United States Brings a WTO Case Against China's Rare Earth Policies

On March 13, 2012, President Obama announced that the United States, Japan, and the EU were jointly initiating a WTO case against China's restrictive policies on rare earths, as well as on tungsten and molybdenum, stating:

> Being able to manufacture advanced batteries and hybrid cars in America is too important for us to stand by and do nothing. We've got to take control of our energy future, and we can't let that energy industry take root in some other country because they were allowed to break the rules.[101]

A USTR factsheet on the dispute listed hybrid and conventional vehicles, advanced electronics, wind turbines, energy efficient lighting, steel, oil and gas, chemicals, and medical equipment as U.S. industries affected by China's export restrictions.[102] USTR Ron Kirk stated that China's export restraints are becoming more restrictive, resulting "in massive distortions and harmful disruptions in supply chains for these materials throughout the global marketplace."[103] According to EU Trade Commissioner Karel De Gucht: "China's restrictions on rare earths and other products violate international trade rules and must be removed. These measures hurt our producers and consumers in the EU and across the world, including manufacturers of pioneering hi-tech and 'green' business applications."[104]

According to the request for consultations with China filed by the United States, Japan, and the EU in the WTO, the following issues have been raised in regards to China's restrictions on rare earths, tungsten, and molybdenum:

- export duties;

- quantitative restrictions, such as quotas;

---

[98] USW, *Petition for Relief Under Section 301 of the1974 Trade Act as Amended, China's Policies Affecting Trade and Investment in Green Technology*, September 9, 2010, p. 23

[99] Because of its WTO obligations, the United States generally must use the WTO's dispute resolution mechanism to resolve trade disputes with other WTO members.

[100] USTR, *2012 Trade Policy Agenda and 2011 Annual Report*, March 1, 2012, p.175.

[101] The White House, *Remarks by the President on Fair Trade*, Rose Garden, March 13, 2012.

[102] USTR, Factsheet, titled "United States Launches WTO Action on Access to Materials Vital to the 21st Century Economy," March 13, 2012.

[103] USTR, Press Release, *United States Challenges China's Export Restraints on Rare Earths at the World Trade Organization*, March 13, 2012.

[104] European Commission, Press Release, *EU Challenges China's Rare Earth Export Restrictions*, March 13, 2012.

- additional requirements and procedures imposed on quantitative restrictions, such as fees and formalities, restrictions on the right to export (such as prior export experience and minimum capital requirements), and other conditions that appear to treat foreign-invested firms different from domestic entities; and

- the maintenance of a minimum export price system and requirements for the examination and approval of export contracts and export prices by Chinese government entities in a manner that is not uniform, impartial, reasonable, and transparent.

A Similar WTO Case on Raw Materials

The WTO dispute case jointly brought by the United States, Japan, and EU is very similar to a WTO case brought by the United States (as well as EU and Mexico) against China in 2009 over its export restrictions on raw materials.[105] The restrictions in question included export quotas, export duties, minimum export price requirements, export licensing, and export quota administration requirements on certain raw materials (including, bauxite, coke, fluorspar, magnesium, manganese, silicon metal, silicon carbide, yellow phosphorus, and zinc).[106] The United States charged that such policies were intended to lower prices for Chinese firms (especially in the steel, aluminum, and chemical sectors) in order to help them obtain an unfair competitive advantage. According to the USTR, such export restraints can "artificially increase world prices for these raw material inputs while artificially lowering prices for Chinese producers. This enables China's domestic downstream producers to produce lower-priced products from the raw materials and thereby creates significant advantages for China's producers when competing against U.S. and other producers both in China's market and other countries' markets. The export restraints can also create substantial pressure on foreign downstream producers to move their operations and, as a result, their technologies to China."[107]

In July 2011, a WTO panel ruled that China's export quotas and duties on certain raw materials violated its WTO commitments. The panel ruled that the wording of China's Protocol of Accession to the WTO did not allow China to use certain general exceptions provided in the WTO agreement to justify its WTO-inconsistent export duties (see **Text Box**). The panel further ruled that even if China could rely on such provisions, it still failed to demonstrate how export restrictions were justified by reasons of conservation of exhaustible natural resources, the prevention of critical shortages, or the reduction of pollution. For example, on the issue of exhaustible resources, China failed to show that it had imposed similar restrictions on domestic production or consumption of raw materials. The panel also found that certain aspects of China's export licensing regime were also inconsistent with WTO rules.

---

[105] Various press reports indicate that the United States, Japan, and EU held off bringing a WTO dispute case against China on rare earths until after the WTO had ruled on China's restrictions on certain raw materials.

[106] The European Union and Mexico became co-complainants to the case, and several other WTO members joined as third parties in the dispute.

[107] USTR, *Press Release*, July 11, 2011.

China's Attempt to Justify its Export Restrictions in the WTO Dispute Settlement Case on Raw Materials

China has argued that its export restrictions are consistent with its obligations under WTO rules. In the WTO case brought by the United States and other WTO members on China's restrictions on certain raw materials, China sought to justify its export duties and quotas based on two main provisions of the General Agreement on Tariffs and Trade 1994 (GATT 1994): Article XX and Article XI:2(a).[108]

Article XX of GATT provides 10 exceptions (paragraphs a to j) to GATT obligations as long as certain requirements are met. Such measures include those necessary to protect human, animal or plant life or health (paragraph b); and those relating to the conservation of exhaustible natural resources if such measures are made effective in conjunction with restrictions on domestic production or consumption (paragraph g). Such restrictions cannot be applied in a manner which would constitute a means of arbitrary or unjustifiable discrimination between countries where the same conditions prevail, or a disguised restriction on international trade. Article XI:2(a) of the GATT enables members to temporarily apply export prohibitions or restrictions to prevent or relieve critical shortages of products essential to the exporting contracting party.[109]

The WTO Panel that was appointed to hear the dispute examined China's export duties in light of Paragraph 11.3 of China's Accession Protocol, which states that "China shall eliminate all taxes and charges applied to exports unless specifically provided for in Annex 6 of this Protocol or applied in conformity with the provisions of Article VIII of the GATT 1994."[110] Annex 6 lists "products subject to export duty" and the maximum export duty rate for each product. A total of 84 different products are listed. China stated it would only raise these duties under "exceptional circumstances."[111] The WTO panel determined that there is no basis in China's Accession Protocol to allow the application of Article XX (b) or (g) of the GATT 1994 to China's obligations in Paragraph 11.3 of the Accession Protocol.[112] The WTO Panel further noted that even if China were entitled to invoke Article XX for imposed export duties and quotas on certain raw materials, it did it not comply with the requirements of those exceptions.[113] It also determined that China's export quotas on certain raw materials could not be justified under GATT Article XI:2(a) because China failed to prove that such measures were applied on a "temporary basis" to either prevent or relieve a "critical shortage." (These two findings were upheld by the Appellate Body.)

Source: WTO.

China appealed the WTO panel's ruling. However, on January 30, 2012, a WTO Appellate Body affirmed that China's export quotas and export taxes on certain raw materials violated its WTO commitments.[114] U.S. Trade Representative Ron Kirk called the decision a "tremendous victory

---

[108] GATT 1994 is part of the WTO agreements.

[109] For additional information on these provisions, see CRS Report R42373, *Issues in International Trade Law: Restricting Exports of Electronic Waste*, by Emily C. Barbour.

[110] Article VIII states in part that import and export fees shall be limited in amount to the approximate cost of services rendered and shall not represent an indirect protection to domestic products or a taxation of imports or exports for fiscal purposes.

[111] Of the raw materials in question in the case, only yellow phosphorus is listed in Annex 6. The panel found that China had removed the special 50% on yellow phosphorus before the panel was established and that the duty was now being imposed at the WTO-consistent rate.

[112] That is, China can only charge export duties on the 84 products (and rates) listed in Annex 6 of the accession agreement and cannot impose export duties on other products. It cannot invoke Article XX of the GATT to impose new duties because China's WTO accession agreement did not specifically state that it could.

[113] For example, the WTO Panel ruled that Article XX(g) permits trade measures relating to conservation of exhaustible natural resources. However, "restrictions on domestic production or consumption must not only be applied jointly with the challenged export restrictions but, in addition, the purpose of those export restrictions must be to ensure the effectiveness of those domestic restrictions." The Appellate Body modified this to state that Article XX(g) permits trade measures relating to conservation of exhaustible natural resources "if such trade measures work together with restrictions on domestic production or consumption, which operate so as to conserve an exhaustible natural resource."

[114] The Appellate Body declared moot and of no legal effect the Panel's findings regarding China's export licensing requirements, minimum export price requirements, administration and allocation of export quotas, and fees and formalities in connection with exportation because of inadequacies in the complainants' panel requests involving these (continued...)

---

for the United States," and that it would ensure that "core manufacturing industries in this country can get the materials they need to produce and compete on a level playing field."[115]

Many analysts speculate that the United States and other major users of rare earths (such as the EU and Japan) were waiting to see how the WTO would rule on the raw materials case before proceeding, noting that many of the export restrictions raised by the United States in the raw materials WTO case (such as export duties and quotas) are similar to those that are imposed by China on raw earths, as well as in regards to the arguments China has made to justify such restrictions (e.g., concerns over pollution and conservation of exhaustible natural resources).

Rare Earths as a Political Weapon?

Many analysts have raised concerns that China sees its control over rare earths as a potential bargaining chip that can be used to gain political and economic advantages over other countries. For example, on September 8, 2010, a collision occurred between a Chinese fishing boat with two Japanese Coast Guard vessels in disputed waters claimed by both countries. The arrest of the Chinese captain by Japanese authorities resulted in a major diplomatic dispute between the two countries.[116] China cut off high-level exchanges with Japan and reportedly threatened to take "strong countermeasures."[117] On September 22, 2010, the New York Times reported that China had begun halting exports of rare earths to Japan. On September 24, Japan agreed to release the Chinese captain. However, on October 19, 2010, the New York Times reported that China's embargo of rare earth exports to Japan appeared to be still in effect and was possibly extended to some rare earth shipments to the United States and the European Union, although China denied such reports.[118] On November 19, 2010, the New York Times reported that China's rare earth exports to Japan had resumed, although with some delays.[119] Chinese trade data show that its rare earth exports to Japan in October and November 2010 were down sharply over previous months in 2010, but rose sharply in December 2010 (see **Figure 10).**

China's alleged efforts to use its control of rare earths as a bargaining chip has prompted concern in the West. In an October 17, 2010 editorial, Paul Krugman stated that the temporary Chinese embargo of rare earth exports to Japan:

(...continued)
measures.

[115] USTR, *Press Release*, January 31, 2012.

[116] For additional information on the incident, see CRS Report RL33436, *Japan-U.S. Relations: Issues for Congress*, coordinated by Emma Chanlett-Avery, p 7.

[117] *The New York Times*, "Arrest in Disputed Seas Riles China and Japan," September 19, 2010.

[118] *The New York Times* article speculated that the alleged Chinese action to limit rare earth exports to the United States was the result of an announcement by the U.S. Trade Representative (USTR) on October 15, 2010, that it had initiated an investigation of China's trade and investment policies on green technologies (*New York Times*, "China Said to Widen Its Embargo of Minerals," October 19, 2010). *Knowledge Wharton* speculated that the restrictions against the United States and the EU were a reflection Beijing's displeasure about the awarding of the Nobel Peace Prize on October 8, 2010 to Chinese dissident Liu Xiaobo (see *Knowledge Wharton*, "A Chinese Wake-Up Call on Rare Earth," December 8, 2010.) According to China's trade data, its rare earth exports (measured according to HTS 2846, 280530, and 360690 commodities) fell from 605 metric tons in September 2010 to 100 metric tons in October, and rose to 205 metric tons in November and to 591 metric tons in December 2010. However, U.S. trade data do not indicate a major decline rare earth imports in late 2010.

[119] *The New York Times*, "China Restarts Rare Earth Shipments to Japan," November 17, 2010.

... shows a Chinese government that is dangerously trigger-happy, willing to wage economic warfare on the slightest provocation...Couple the rare earth story with China's behavior on other fronts — the state subsidies that help firms gain key contracts, the pressure on foreign companies to move production to China and, above all, that exchange-rate policy — and what you have is a portrait of a rogue economic superpower, unwilling to play by the rules. [120]

In a October 7, 2010 speech, Chinese Premier Wen Jiabao stated:

We haven't imposed, and will not, impose an embargo on the industry. We are pursuing a sustainable development of the rare earth industry, not only to meet the demand of our own country, but also to cater to the needs of the whole world. We not only need to accommodate the current demand, but also, more significantly, need to take a long-term perspective. It is necessary to exercise management and control over the rare earth industry, but there won't be any embargo. China is not using rare earth as a bargaining chip. We aim for the world's sustainable development. [121]

Figure 10. Chinese Monthly Rare Earth Exports to Japan in 2010

(metric tons)

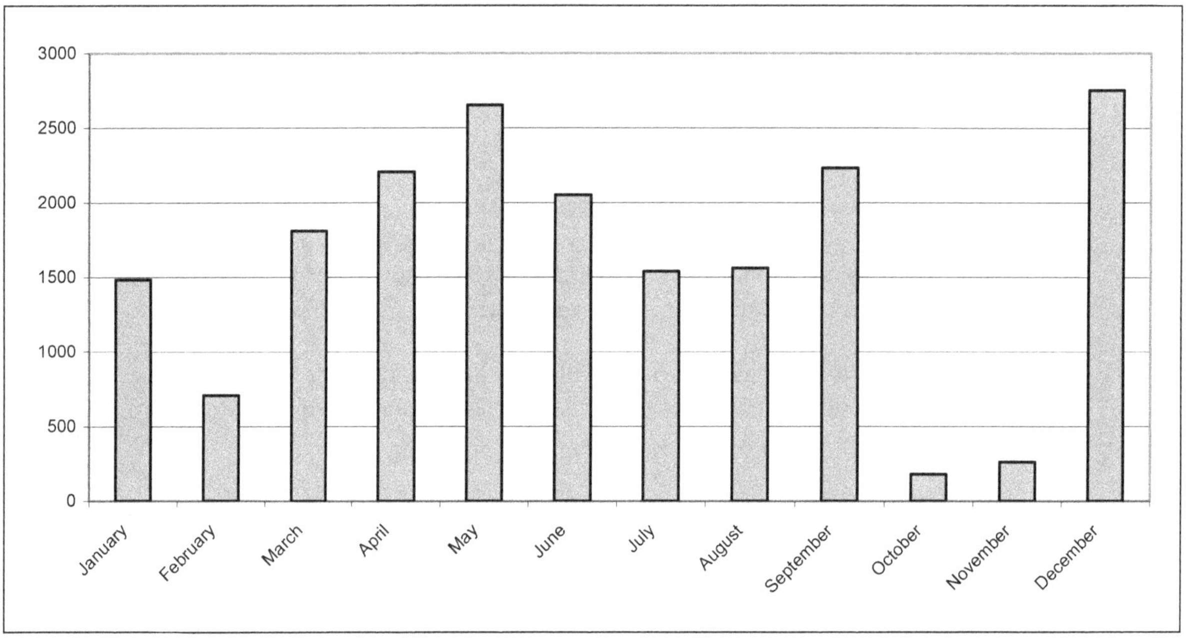

Source: World Trade Atlas.

Note: Rare earth data in this figure reflect Chinese exports of harmonized tariff code numbers 2846, 280530, and 360690.

---

[120] *The New York Times*, "Rare and Foolish," October 17, 2010.

[121] Xinhua, "Premier Wen's Speech at Sixth China-EU Business Summit," October 7, 2010.

Issues for Congress

Congressional Response

At least 14 bills have been introduced in Congress that would attempt to address the availability of rare earths (and other materials and elements) for U.S. industries (including defense-related industries) and lessening U.S. dependence on China, through such measures as promoting the research and development (R&D) of rare earth resources and related industries in the United States.[122] In November 2011, Representatives Hank Johnson and Mike Coffman announced the formation of a congressional Rare Earth Caucus.[123] According to Representative Coffman: "With the establishment of this caucus, I am confident we will be able to build awareness on Capitol Hill about the critical threat China's trade policies of restricting rare earth exports pose to both the economic and national security of the United States."[124] A March 2011 letter written by Senators Casey, Schumer, Stabenow, and Whitehouse urged the Obama Administration to instruct the U.S. Executive Director at each multilateral bank, including the World Bank, to oppose the approval of any new financing to the Chinese government for rare earth projects in China, including rare earth mining, smelting or separation, or production of rare earth products.[125] The letter also urged the Administration to impose the same types of restrictions on Chinese investment in mineral exploration and purchases in the United States as China imposes on foreign investment in rare earths in China.[126]

During his State of the Union Address on January 24, 2012, President Obama announced plans to create a Trade Enforcement Unit that will be "charged with investigating unfair trade practices in countries like China."[127] In February 2012, Congressman Mike Coffman and nine other Members sent a letter to President Obama noting the WTO Panel's and Appellate Body's rulings on China's restrictions on raw materials, and stating that:

> The similarity between Chinese raw material exports and rare earth exports suggests that rectifying the rare earth situation should be among the first efforts undertaken in any new focus on trade equality." We urge you to point the new Trade Enforcement Unit at various restrictions, quotas, and de facto embargos used by China in the rare earth market. Many of us have also urged a WTO case against China due to their rare earth practices, and we renew that request with you as well.[128]

---

[122] A listing and description of these bills can be found at CRS Report R41744, *Rare Earth Elements in National Defense: Background, Oversight Issues, and Options for Congress*, by Valerie Bailey Grasso; and CRS Report R41347, *Rare Earth Elements: The Global Supply Chain*, by Marc Humphries.

[123] At the time of the announcement, the caucus had 15 members.

[124] Representative Mike Coffman Press Release, November 9, 2011.

[125] The letter states that "the United States should not sit passively while China's investment policies hamstring U.S. companies and undermine our national and economic security needs."

[126] The letter can be found at http://casey.senate.gov/newsroom/press/release/print.cfm?id=81a1fa95-49d2-47a7-98b4-65973ae14ddc.

[127] On February 28, 2012, President Obama by executive order created a new Interagency Trade Enforcement Center, which will, among other things, "serve as the primary forum within the Federal Government for USTR and other agencies to coordinate enforcement of U.S. trade rights under international trade agreements and enforcement of domestic trade laws."

[128] The letter is available at http://coffman.house.gov/images/stories/coffmanlettertowhitehouseonchinaretradepolicy2-2-2012.pdf.

Agency Reports on Rare Earth Supplies

In 2010 and 2011, the Department of Energy issued a Critical Materials Strategy report, which examines the role that rare earth metals and other key materials play in clean energy technologies. The 2011 report found that several clean energy technologies, including wind turbines, electric vehicles (EVs), photovoltaic (PV) thin films, fluorescent lighting, use materials at risk of supply disruptions in the short term (present-2015), although those risks are expected to decrease in the medium-and-long terms, and that supply challenges for five rare earth metals (dysprosium, neodymium, terbium, europium and yttrium) may affect clean energy technology deployment in the years ahead. [129] Other elements, including cerium, indium, lanthanum and tellurium, were estimated to be near-critical between the short and the medium-term (2015–2025). The report further states that DOE's strategy for addressing critical materials challenges is based on three pillars, including: (1) the development of diversified global rare earth supply chains (including mining, extraction, processing, and manufacturing in the United States and abroad) in order to reduce supply risks that occur from China's position as the dominant producer of rare earth supplies; (2) the development of substitutes, including through government-sponsored research; and (3) recycling, reuse and more efficient use rare earths. In addition, DOE has indicated that it has organized a number of workshops with the European Union, Japan, Australia and Canada to identify possible R&D collaboration efforts.

An April 2012 report by the Department of Defense (DoD) provided a relatively optimistic assessment of the ability of U.S. defense industries that use rare earths to meet their supply needs.[130] Of the seven rare earth materials identified as the most prevalent among defense consumption for the purposes of procurement (dysprosium, erbium, europium, gadolinium, neodymium, praseodymium, and yttrium), DoD determined that by 2013, U.S. production of rare earth materials could satisfy U.S. consumption required to meet defense procurement needs, with the exception of yttrium. The report stated that market forces in the United States and globally have led to falling prices, increased investments and domestic supply of rare earth materials, corporate restructuring within the supply chain, and technical advances, which, as a result, are "trending positive for a market capable of meeting future U.S. Government demand."[131]

Implications of the WTO Case on Rare Earths

To many observers, China's rare earth restrictions are representative of a series of government interventionist policies that have been implemented in recent years that attempt to pick winners and losers in the marketplace, often occurring, it is argued, at the expense of the economic interests of other countries. Such critics contend that China's policy to sharply limit rare earth exports is intended to make Chinese domestic firms the dominant producer and supplier of global renewable energy products and/or to induce foreign firms to move production to China and to transfer technology to Chinese firms as the price for a reliable supply of rare earths. Many

---

[129] U.S. Department of Energy, *Critical Materials Strategy*, December 2011, available at http://energy.gov/sites/prod/files/DOE_CMS2011_FINAL_Full.pdf.

[130] DoD was required by section 843 of the National Defense Authorization Act For Fiscal Year 2011 (P.L. 111-383) to assess which, if any, rare earth materials are (1) critical to the production, sustainment, or operation of significant United States military equipment, and (2) which of these are subject to interruption of supply, based on actions or events outside the control of the U.S. government.

[131] U.S. Department of Defense, Under Secretary of Defense for Acquisition, Technology, and Logistics, *Report to Congress on, Rare Earth Materials in Defense Applications*, March 2012.

contend that such policies violate China's WTO obligations and argue that more WTO dispute settlement cases should be brought against China to challenge such practices.

The WTO case against China's rare earth policies that was jointly filed by the United States, EU, and Japan appear to indicate a degree of cooperation among some of the world's largest economies, which also constitute China's largest trading partners.[132] Some might argue that such a united front might convey to China the seriousness to which such countries view China's rare earth restrictions, and that they might also cooperate to take other actions against China's rare earth policies beyond the scope of the WTO case.

The WTO case against China's rare earth restrictions raises a number of questions:

- If the WTO ruled largely in the favor of the United States, EU, and Japan and found that the restrictions that were cited are inconsistent with China's WTO obligations, would China implement those findings in a timely manner?

- Would China implement the "spirit" of the WTO's to remove such restrictions (such as export duties and quotas) or would it seek to implement other restrictions that would be more complicated to challenge in the WTO?

- Even if the United States, EU, and Japan prevailed in the dispute, would China's compliance with the WTO's findings be implemented in a timely manner or would it try to delay changes to its rare earth export regime?

- Are there alternatives for dealing with China's rare earth export restrictions apart from the current WTO dispute resolution case? For example, could the Chinese government be induced to allow foreign companies to mine rare earths in China if such firms helped to improve environmental mining conditions in China (which China claims is a major factor behind its rare earth policies) in exchange for a guarantee that a certain quantity of rare earths could be exported?

The WTO case on certain raw materials that was brought against China by the United States was initiated in June 2009. In July 2011, a WTO panel issued a report of its findings. China then appealed, and in January 2012, a WTO Appellate Body issued its findings. As of the time of this writing, China has not indicated how and when it intends to implement the Appellate Body's findings.[133] This has led some to contend the WTO case against China on rare earths may have come too late for U.S. firms that are currently dealing with relatively high rare earth prices, and thus, it is argued, the WTO case may do little to prevent U.S. high tech firms (as well as those in Japan and the EU) from moving their production to China.[134] Other analysts argue that, while there have been anecdotal evidence that some rare earth users may have established or expanded operations in China, there is no evidence of a large-scale flight of foreign firms to China because of Chinese rare earth policies. Other analysts note that China's restrictions on rare earths may have backfired somewhat because such restrictions led to a sharp decline in global demand for rare earths and thus caused a sharp decline in prices during the second half of 2011 and the first few months of 2012.

---

[132] The WTO submissions filed by the United States, the EU, and Japan were nearly identical.

[133] For an overview of the WTO dispute settlement process, see CRS Report RS20088, *Dispute Settlement in the World Trade Organization (WTO): An Overview*, by Jeanne J. Grimmett.

[134] *The New York Times*, "Specialists in Rare Earths Say a Trade Case Against China May Be Too Late," March 14, 2012.

Concluding Thoughts

The timing issue has also been raised regarding the development of alternative sources of rare earths, including those mined in the United States, Australia, and elsewhere. Many analysts argue that it could take years to make a significant dent in China's near monopoly of rare earths. Others contend that mining rare earths is not enough as long as China is the dominant processor of rare earth elements and a major manufacturer of rare earth products, such as magnets. Some have suggested that certain types of heavy rare earths can be only processed in China. This creates a potential scenario where a U.S. firm that mines, or obtains certain heavy rare earths from non-Chinese sources, must send its rare earths to China, where, ironically, they would be subject to Chinese export restraints.

Yet, it is not clear under what market conditions (e.g., prices and supply) would make it commercially viable for non-Chinese firms to engage in downstream sectors that would generate a rare earth supply chain independent of China. According to the General Accountability Office (GAO), rebuilding a U.S. rare earth supply chain could take up to 15 years and is dependent on several factors, including securing capital investments in processing infrastructure, developing new technologies, and acquiring patents, which are currently held by international companies.[135]

This has further raised questions as to what role the federal government should play (if any) in leading and possibly financing efforts to reestablish a U.S. rare earth supply chain, and/or to support efforts through R&D to help U.S. firms that are downstream users of rare earths to improve the efficiency of their use, recycle, or develop alternative materials as a way to lessen U.S. dependence on China for these materials.[136]

Author Contact Information

Wayne M. Morrison
Specialist in Asian Trade and Finance
wmorrison@crs.loc.gov, 7-7767

Rachel Tang
Analyst in Asian Affairs
rtang@crs.loc.gov, 7-7875

---

[135] GAO, *Rare Earth Materials in the Defense Supply Chain*, April 14, 2010, p. 13, at http://www.gao.gov/new.items/d10617r.pdf

[136] Some analysts contend that Chinese officials welcome efforts by foreign countries and firms to develop alternative sources of rare earths because of Chinese concerns that in a few years domestic production will not be able to keep up with domestic demand, which could force China to become a rare earths importer in the near future.